Kudos for *The Blades*

"[The author] writes a memoir/history book about not only his experiences as a U.S. Army Chinook helicopter pilot in Vietnam — one of the finer books on ... helicopter activity in that war — but also as a humanist and his reactions to the war ... A thrilling suspenseful adventure [story] and a bow to the constancy of marriages that survived.... Highly Recommend."

–Grady Harp *Amazon Hall of Fame Top 500 Reviewer*

"The tone retains the spirit of spontaneity; confidence, competitiveness, and humor inherent in youth ... The scenes in Vietnam present a tight and convincing package of what it was like to fly the Chinook in combat."

–Henry Zeybel, *Vietnam Veterans of America*

"[The authors] have written a book that is unique when it comes to a memoir of the Vietnam War....[It's] a well written and engaging reading experience and I highly recommend it."

–John Penny for *The VHPA Aviator Vietnam Helicopter Pilots Association*

"I still have butterflies.... *The Blades Carry Me* is a unique contribution to the great body of Vietnam War literature. I especially recommend it to anyone curious about the human beings who fought the war because in this book one experiences the entire spectrum of human personality."

–Robbie Grayson III, *Traitmaker* Founder/CEO

"Weatherill reconstructed the dialogue authentically, with the lingo (and larger issues) of that unique time and place."

—John P. Jones III, *Amazon Top 1000 Reviewer Vine Voice*

"The Things They Carried, a collection of short stories about a platoon of American soldiers in Vietnam, was a finalist for a Pulitzer Prize. *The Blades Carry Me...* is as good."

—Jan W. Steenblik, Technical Editor, *Air Line Pilots Association International*

"The ... authors ... take turns telling their part of the story, which is intertwined like dancers moving effortless together, then apart, then together again."

—Judge, *22nd Annual Writer's Digest Self-Published Book Awards*

THE BLADES CARRY ME

THE BLADES CARRY ME

ME

INSIDE THE HELICOPTER WAR IN VIETNAM

James V. Weatherill

with

Anne Weatherill

WXILLWORDS PRESS
THE BLADES CARRY ME: INSIDE THE HELICOPTER WAR IN
VIETNAM
James V. Weatherill with Anne Weatherill

Cover photo courtesy of Jerry Sears.
Map of Vietnam drawn by James V. Weatherill.
Chinook logo from a photograph taken by James V. Weatherill.

Published in the United States by WxillWords Press

Library of Congress Control Number: 2014903147
ISBN 978-0-9915430-0-7 (Paperback)
ISBN 978-0-9915430-1-4 (eBook)

Printed by CreateSpace, a DBA of On-Demand Publishing, LLC

To those who came home, those who didn't,
and those who waited

James V. Weatherill in Vietnam

Map of Vietnam

DMZ

Da Nang

LAOS

Dak Pek

BenHet Dak To

T Bone

Dog Bone

Kontum Tara

Timberline

Pleiku AnKhe Qui Nhon

CAMBODIA

Tuy Hoa

Otis Phu Hiep

Ban Me Thout

Duc Lap

Bu Krak Nha Trang

Dalat Cam Ranh Bay

VIETNAM Phan Rang

Phan Thiet

Long Binh

Saigon Vung Tao SOUTH CHINA SEA

Contents

Part 5: March 1968
265 Days to Go

Part 6: April 1968
234 Days to Go

Part 7: May 1968
204 Days to Go

Part 8: June 1968
173 Days to Go

Part 9: July 1968
143 Days to Go

Part 10: August 1968
112 Days to Go

Part 11: September 1968
81 Days to Go

Part 12: October 1968
51 Days to Go

Part 13: November 1968
20 Days to Go

Author's Notes

My purpose is to promote awareness of the contributions of Chinook helicopter crews to the Vietnam War and aviation history.

People and events are based on my recollections, flight records, letters, tapes, and experience as an Army CH-47 Chinook helicopter pilot in Vietnam. Missions flown and living conditions depicted are typical for personnel at that time. I apologize for timelines that may be off.

Chinook pilots normally did not have individual call signs. Instead, they used the helicopters' tail numbers. To avoid confusion I chose to assign a personal call sign to the pilots and myself.

People are composites. Conversations are re-created and represent the way we spoke. Names and identifying characteristics are changed to protect each person's privacy and right to tell his own story.

Military families who support their service members from afar have their own untold stories. Annie, my wife, agreed to add her perspective for the year she waited.

Four and a half decades is a long, emotional journey back, and memories are fallible, even blank at times, no matter the prodding. Together, Annie and I gathered the strength to open the footlocker of letters and tapes we had kept all these years. In the process, we exorcised some ghosts and now understand better what happened to each of us in 1968.

Acknowledgements

Cover photo

Jerry Sears took the cover photo during the movement of a firebase in the Central Highlands of Vietnam in 1968. A CH-47A Chinook helicopter removes a cannon and an ammo piggyback load. Charred and collapsed bunkers bear witness to the magnitude of the battle fought on this ground.

Preparation of vintage slides and cover and logo designs courtesy of David Satterwhite.

In appreciation

Thank you to Charles Donahue; Cathy and Dennis Foose; Cmdr. Robert E. Forest, USN, retired; Robbie Grayson III; Roger Lesch; Jonathan Payne; Gretchen R. Ray; Alan Rinzler; Karl Rubinstein; Capt. Charles Savournin; Gil and Col. Marie Moore Shelden, US Army, retired; Jean and Lt.Col. Larry Whipple, USMC, retired.

The war comes like a thin blade cutting;
Slicing like a draft at the doors of our lives.
We use our youth to block its way.

PART 1
NOVEMBER 1967

Letting Go and Hanging On

Riverside, California

Annie and I are at my parents' home, in the bedroom where my older brother and I shared adolescent dreams and secrets, and planned grand adventures. A balsa wood plane still dangles from the ceiling above the bed on my side of the room.

"There, did you feel it?" Beneath the covers, Annie presses my hand tighter against her belly.

"No," I say, bemused by the thought that somebody no bigger than my thumb could make enough commotion to be felt from outside. I snuggle my chest against Annie's spine and breathe into the back of her neck. "It's probably just gas."

Her elbow shoots back and wings me in the ribs. Her belly transmits a fleeting series of thumps to the palm of my hand.

"God, it *is* real!" I lean into her, pushed by solid wonder.

I feel her body stiffen, and in a choked whisper she says, "He's part of you that will stay here with me—that I can hang onto. He'll have your smile and your licorice curls."

But I envision a skinny little girl with strawberry-blonde hair and a sprinkle of freckles; a kite tugging at the string in her hand, taunting her to let it join the clouds.

Annie turns over to face me. "You'll come back to us?"

I'm not superstitious, but I'm afraid to answer. I leave tomorrow. I have a ticket to Vietnam in my pocket. My thumb-size ticket to immortality cavorts, oblivious, in my wife's womb. Engulfed by the mystery of it all, I sleep as time circles the earth. In a blink it's tomorrow.

My mother stands in front of the kitchen sink and squints out the window into the bright Southern California morning. She's said less and less as my thirty-day leave counted down to day zero. She lights a filter cigarette and looks at me. "You'll be careful, won't you?" she asks in a husky voice.

"Yeah, Ma, I will." I pick up a plate and stack on some pancakes.

She passes me the syrup. Then, her cigarette hanging from her lips, she fidgets with the rosary in her apron pocket.

"It's okay with me if you wear that rosary out, you know."

"I'm scared, son."

"So am I."

Riverside, California: Annie

Jim and I climb into the family Oldsmobile with his parents and sister. Fred drives and Marie sits in the front passenger seat. I snuggle in the back seat next to Jim. He puts his arm around me and squeezes my shoulder. I lean into his chest. The fabric of his uniform is rough on my cheek.

His sixteen-year-old sister, Janie, sits like granite on the other side of me and stares out the window. She's made it clear she blames me for her brother's half-baked decision to enlist in the middle of a war. But she's wrong; his score on the college deferment exam put him in the bull's-eye for the draft. Enlisting is a preemptive move toward his dream of flying.

Jim and I cling to each other as we move through the small Ontario International Airport terminal. I study his face to burn his essence into my memory. He releases me to give Janie a hug and kiss. Then, he shakes his father's hand. Fred, retired military, salutes, and Jim returns the honor. He grabs me again, and melts me with his embrace and kisses. Then, he turns to his mother.

Marie reaches up to her son. I see pain in her eyes and tension in her body as she struggles with her feelings. She releases Jim and clears her throat. "You will be careful," she commands and pleads simultaneously.

"Yeah, Ma, I will." His eyes moisten, and he turns to climb the stairs to the airplane.

Now, Marie has seen two generations—husband and son—go to war. A step behind, I send my husband off to Vietnam. I pray that someday I will not have to send our child into battle, too.

We stay to watch the airplane lift off, and then we drive back to Riverside, where I will stay with Jim's family while I finish my senior year of college. Fred changes cars and drives to work. Janie takes off with a friend.

"Let's get our hair done," Marie suggests and forces a smile.

A salon Marie frequents coincidentally has two empty chairs. My hairdresser drones on and on about problems with her current boyfriend. How I envy that he is still within her reach, even for the luxury of an argument. I sit with my hands on my belly and concentrate on nudges from the life that combines Jim's DNA and mine.

As I pay at the reception desk, Marie whispers something to the hairdresser. The hairdresser blushes, puts her hand to her mouth, and looks at me as if I had just been diagnosed with some fatal disease. "I'm sorry. I didn't realize," she begins.

"It's okay," I interrupt and bolt for the door.

Somewhere near the International Date Line

The Pacific Ocean gleams with starlight, and the cloudless sky melts into the black water. The flight is already six hours, and we're only halfway across. Soldiers sleep all around me. I close my eyes and recall my journey from college.

I'm in the Army recruiting office in San Bernardino, California, volunteering for helicopter flight school. Two days later, I'm on a loaded Greyhound bus headed for the government induction center in Los Angeles. The first test is given to about 800 of us in a room the size of a high school gymnasium. Half survive for the second test. Day two, I work through flying, cartography and spatial orientation. Day three, the remaining thirty-three of us take a flight physical; seven pass. Then, I'm interviewed by a panel of Army officers. If they decide they want me, I must decide if I want them. We both say yes.

A week earlier, I was a university student on summer break. Now, I'm in line behind the pied piper of last options. I remember the adage, "Be careful what you wish for." I look at the pool of youth around me and realize I've been drawn out in a cup.

Riding on a Southern Airways DC-3, I arrive for basic training at Fort Polk, Louisiana, and 1966 Louisiana "White Only" drinking fountains. Then comes helicopter flight school and gallons of sweat in Mineral Wells, Texas. On leave back in California, I kneel with Annie at the altar—a "2" painted on the soles of my Army shoes visible to the congregation—then take her to Texas.

After a transfer to Fort Rucker, Alabama, for instrument, formation, survival and Huey helicopter training, I receive my wings and commission as a Warrant Officer 1. I'm selected for CH-47 Chinook transition and learn to fly the large, twin engine cargo helicopter. When that training ends, I have thirty days to take care of personal business before I queue up for the Pacific crossing.

A hand shakes my shoulder. "Sir, wake up, please."

"Huh. What's wrong?"

"You were talking in your sleep." The sergeant beside me answers. "Something about flight school. You were getting pretty loud. I thought I should wake you."

Outside, the sun peeks over the horizon behind us. "Where are we?" I ask.

"The stewardess said another five hours to Saigon."

"Five hours, huh? Thanks again for the heads up."

"No problem, Sir. Maybe someday you'll give me a ride in your helicopter."

"Any time."

I doze off and on and wake to pressure pain in my ears. Out my window the water ends, and Asia begins.

Riverside, California: Annie

Our dog, Bonnie, presses her nose to the glass patio door and bites her lip. She refuses to eat. She will not let me out of her sight except for her vigil at the door. I push the door slightly open. Bonnie turns away and politely wags her tail.

I lean down and rub behind her ears. "Good girl, Bon. It's okay," I encourage her.

Her ears perk up, but her eyes are flat.

I kneel down and put my arms around her neck. "Me, too," I whisper in her ear.

Vietnam

Our World Airways plane arrives at the Tan Son Nhut Airport, Saigon, Republic of Vietnam, give or take the International Date Line, the day before Thanksgiving 1967; Vietnam, the new mailing address, the new order, the Far East under my feet. Welcome to grinding gears and revving engines; blue and black exhaust clouds from

every machine; paved and dirt streets crammed with
people on bicycles and old Lambretta motor-scooters;
storefront signs with letters that baffle me; people
speaking a sing-song language.

Welcome to life recycled: homes sheathed with
discarded aluminum; lamps from howitzer casings;
children's kites from parachute panels dyed red, green,
gold; people in blue, black, yellow and white clothes that
look like silky, airy, pajamas; round pyramid hats made of
reeds, and sandals from old tire tread.

Welcome to a stench that rides the wind and makes
us new guys cough and gag; life in a malaria-filled Asian
purgatory where some might never get cured. Fixed wing
aircraft mix with helicopters overhead. Razor sharp coils
of concertina wire encircle our compounds, gun positions
every hundred feet, minefields, trip-flares, board
sidewalks like Atlantic City. Sandbags piled around beds
make blinds from night fights and whistling mortars.

Welcome to the distortion of waking crazed and not
knowing if the dream is really over, mixed with whiskey,
86-proof relief in $2 bottles—a volatile norm.

Your age doesn't matter. Nothing matters except
breathing, and air is normally drawn through a tobacco
tube of some sort. Yeah, welcome to Southeast Asia.

Pacing in transient hooches, sleeping quarters, I
watch insects crawl across floors—large insects with
unknown names. The sun is bright, but I don't notice
until night, and night is filled with longing.

Riding helicopters and fixed wing aircraft, I work my
way in country through Saigon, Long Binh, Phan Thiet,
Nha Trang, Tuy Hoa, and finally land in Phu Hiep.
Having been three days in country, I get to the 180th
Assault Support Helicopter Company.

In my descent into Vietnam, people who befriended
me during our journey from America are cut from our
group: three in Long Binh, slice; four more in Phan Thiet,
slice; two in Nha Trang and then only me. Now, no one
knows my name. I feel invisible.

"Mister Weatherill?" a corporal asks as I step off the Huey that deposits me and my baggage in Phu Hiep.

"What?"

"Are you Mister Weatherill?"

"I am."

"Please follow me, Sir. I'll take you to the transient hooch. You'll in-process tomorrow morning. They'll move you to permanent hooch later." My footlocker still in transit somewhere, the corporal swings my duffel-bag onto his shoulder.

"Any place to get some food, Corporal?" I ask, looking around in the dark.

"I'll take you to the mess, Sir. It's after hours but I'll get you some sandwiches. You can get a drink at the officers' bar. I'll take you there, too. Almost all the crews are away on missions, but the bar is always open. It's sort of a tradition."

I follow the corporal, like a puppy with a new master, to my temporary quarters and drop my duffel. Then we go to the mess, where I inhale two ham sandwiches.

"What would you like, Sir?" the corporal asks, as we enter the officers' bar.

"Scotch, please."

He pours me a glass of scotch and I take it back to the transient hooch. I nurse it as long as I can before I fall asleep.

In the morning, I walk into an unfamiliar routine. I feel fully grown but that I know nothing. Then life changes. They hand me a pistol, a survival kit and different colored malaria pills. I get a cloth "blood chit," with an image of a U.S. flag and a notice in dozens of languages offering a reward to anyone who offers aid if I'm shot down. There's more: a flak jacket, a chest plate designed to slow down bullets, a ballistic flight helmet and plastic maps.

Seven days from lying in my wife's arms and feeling my immortality, I'm flying with an instructor pilot, learning how to sling load a cannon from one firebase to another. Seven days from my small, growing family, to bullets and mortars and trying not to die from small new-guy mistakes.

Riverside, California: Annie

It's been eight days since Jim's departure. He's somewhere in Vietnam now. His absence creates a palpable void that demands to be filled. I've already written several letters. His family and I eagerly await his letters and tape recordings. It's understood that I'll share with his parents his communications to me. It seems a fair exchange for a place to stay, and my Italian mother-in-law will make sure I eat regularly. We will joyfully welcome evidence that Jim was fine when he sent his letters and tapes, but brace ourselves for the anxiety of not knowing how he is at the moment we read or hear his words.

Jim's father and I have become news junkies with insatiable cravings for tangible connections to him. We grasp at any information. Television newscasts, the newspaper boy and the mailman are our suppliers. Each evening, transfixed by monochrome flickers of the television screen, we sit on the couch, and Bonnie lies on Fred's feet. We cringe at ads for feminine hygiene products and hemorrhoid relief as we scan each broadcast with hope and dread for even a glimpse of Jim. Unsuccessful, we are torn between relief and dismay.

Today, I spot a headline in the newspaper. A Chinook was shot down. I give the paper to Fred when he gets home from work. He glances at the headline and takes the paper to his bedroom.

PART 2

DECEMBER 1967

356 DAYS TO GO

2

The Way It Works

Vietnam

A common wall of concertina wire joins our base to the west side of the village of Phu Hiep. East of Phu Hiep is the South China Sea, north is Tuy Hoa Air Force Base, and south is a contingent of Koreans with the White Horse Division. The base lies halfway down the coast of South Vietnam from the DMZ (the demilitarized zone between North and South Vietnam), or up the coast from Saigon, depending on how you look at a map.

Our hooches are made of lapstrake wood planking with corrugated steel roofs and mosquito netting at the eaves. Hooch numbers are stenciled on screen doors. The hooches wrap like a giant U around a sand courtyard. At the base of the U is a breezeway shortcut to the operations room and the remainder of the company area.

Interior furnishings are basic government: a gray wall locker without a lock and a green tube-frame bed with steel springs and a three-inch thick mattress. A cupboard between the beds holds a small white sink, with cold water available a couple hours each day. Walls and floors are plywood.

Pilots in our company are split into two platoons, each led by a captain. Above the platoon leaders are majors in charge of operations, administration and maintenance. The executive officer is also a major, and our commanding officer is a lieutenant colonel. Enlisted soldiers have the same administrative structure with different level sergeants. We warrant officers are subordinate to lieutenants and just above the highest enlisted grade. We hover in between.

Each officer has an additional duty, such as motor pool officer, supply officer or operations officer. The job of indigenous personnel officer lands on me; it becomes my job to keep track of about twenty Vietnamese nationals working for our helicopter company. Some jobs, such as pay officer, officer of the day, and tactical emergency crew, are assigned on a rotation basis. Everyone keeps track of the Tactical Emergency List because these are missions flown in dire situations: a wartime "Dial-O-for-Operator" response team for ammo, guns and soldiers.

Our company has sixteen Chinook helicopters. The Chinook is a transport category helicopter manufactured by Boeing Airplane Company. It has two 2,650-horsepower turbine engines and two main rotor systems interconnected by a series of drive shafts so the rotors—overlapping twenty or so feet—won't hit one another while they rotate. It becomes a powered glider if one engine quits and a rock if both engines stop. Including rotor blades, it's more than ninety feet long and can carry 8,000 pounds of cargo internally, externally, or in combination. Normally, we haul supplies externally, in slings under the aircraft. Chinooks are so new we have a Boeing technical representative living with our company.

The Army requires 400 flight hours as a copilot before we can take the tests for aircraft commander. Given we're in a war, it takes three to four months to log the time. It's said that by then we can discuss the Chinook with the Boeing engineers who built it, and we'll know things that not even they know about their machine.

The Chinook is a senior helicopter. In a normal world, the Army wouldn't allow new, inexperienced pilots like me to fly it. Large helicopters are traditionally an incentive for pilot retention. However, difficult times call for innovative choices.

As a new pilot, I fly with "old-timers." Old-timers see the end of their Vietnam tour, and some their Army careers, both counting the days until they return to America. Some have become superstitious and don't want to know new pilots. Old-timers are too short in country and don't want some new-guy mistake to get them killed.

Getting killed isn't limited by anything. It's like fate: tempt enough and you will lose. Being new at anything is nerve-racking, but being new at war ratchets up nerve ends. I keep my new mouth shut and my young eyes open wide.

I strap myself into the right seat of a Chinook for today's firebase move. I have a headache. I ate some aspirin with my powered eggs at the mess hall, and I'm still waiting for them to work.

CW3 Horton climbs in next to me. "Don't touch anything," is all he says. Just his presence takes the wind out of any sail within a fifty-meter radius. He starts the Chinook and we leave the comfort of our revetment, a sandbag walled parking stall, and Phu Hiep.

We're one of four Chinooks on a mission to move pieces of a firebase to a location about fifteen kilometers west. The loads consist of six 105 mm howitzer cannons; the fire control conex full of aiming computers; tons of ammunition; hundreds of men with equipment; food stores, fuel, a Jeep mounted 106 mm recoilless rifle; and anything else necessary to life on a firebase.

 The purpose of a firebase is to provide cannon fire support against the enemy. The move goes fast; I'm getting the rhythm of the coordination and learning the language.

The bullet doesn't make a sound as it enters the open cockpit window. It glances off Horton's ballistic helmet with a sharp pop. His head jerks toward me as the bullet embeds itself in the overhead structure of the cockpit.

"You okay, Horton?"

His eyes look vacant: nobody home.

"Horton!" I yell into the intercom.

We are just short of touching a 105 mm cannon to the ground.

"Down five, Sir," our crew chief instructs while lying on his belly to look through the hook well.

I take control of the aircraft. The cannon lands in its sandbagged circle of its own accord.

"Release, release," the crew chief says.

I electrically release the cannon sling from the helicopter's belly hook. I push the right rudder pedal to turn to our departure heading and add power to climb away from other incoming aircraft. "Horton's been hit. We're returning to base," I broadcast.

"Any damage?" someone asks.

"Nothing obvious."

Through the chin bubble, the cockpit window below my feet, I see two soldiers firing machine guns downhill into the jungle at the perimeter of the firebase.

A Huey, a single engine utility helicopter, unloads four passengers on the base and pulls up alongside our machine. "You look okay from here. We'll check the other side."

Our door gunners hang out their gun ports at the ends of their safety harnesses. "We're okay, Mister Weatherill. No damage left."

"No damage right," comes a second reply.

"We're breaking off, unless you want company," the Huey driver says.

"We're good, thank you."

"What's good?" Horton mutters. "What the hell is going on?"

"You were hit in the helmet. We're going home, get you a medic."

He takes over the controls and command of the aircraft. I take a moment to light a cigarette.

"You prick." Horton grabs the cigarette out of my mouth and takes a deep draw.

"I guess that cigarette makes you a cock sucker by proxy, then."

It goes absolutely quiet in the cockpit. War and a bad temperament. Not even a thank you. But somewhere along the way my headache quit.

When we land at Phu Hiep, I receive a message to visit the mess sergeant as soon as I return to our company area; an indigenous personnel issue has arisen. The mess sergeant has a revolt on his hands.

The tension in the mess hall is solid and hot. A line of six Vietnamese, five workers, and an ancient man in a gold-trimmed black robe stand along the back wall of the kitchen. I'm assailed by the mess sergeant and Mr. Phong, one of our official interpreters.

Mr. Phong wears his usual black slacks, shined black shoes, and starched white shirt. "Thank you for coming, Mister Weatherill," he begins. "It seems, Sir, the workers are afraid of having their blood taken."

"What crap," the mess sergeant says, a cigarette bobbing from his lips.

"Why?" I ask. It makes no sense to me that a simple blood test could cause such a ruckus.

Mr. Phong introduces me to the Buddhist priest standing at the back of the kitchen and relays my question. The man half bows and speaks in a soft voice. It's his belief, and that of the workers, that an American plot is afoot to drain each worker of his blood, one vial at a time.

"Nonsense!" the mess sergeant hisses.

Mr. Phong takes what seems like a minute to relay the sergeant's single word.

"Follow me," I order.

Our procession winds through the compound and enters the front door of the battalion dispensary. I inform the doctor about our problem. Through Mr. Phong, the doctor explains the bloodletting procedure as he takes a vial and a paper cup from a drawer. He fills the vial with water, once for each worker, and pours the water into the cup. It becomes obvious to everyone in the room that the total of all the blood samples would fill the cup.

The priest folds his arms in victory. When he does, I take off my shirt and lie on a stretcher at the side of the room where the doctor extracts a pint of my blood. The priest gasps and harmony returns.

*   *   *

The second cup of 5 a.m. coffee gives me an acid stomach as I walk up to the Chinook for today's sorties. I pile my helmet, chest plate and flak vest on the ramp at the back of our helicopter.

"I'll do the preflight, Mister Weatherill," CW3 Burrows says. "Just take your seat."

"I'd like to watch, if that's all right?"

"I'm not sure you know enough to watch."

"How the hell am I supposed to learn?"

"Learn from someone else. Get aboard."

I climb onto the aft ramp, introduce myself to the crew chief and gunners and settle into the cockpit.

We fly north from Phu Hiep and land in Qui Nhon to refuel. We're to resupply American assets clearing Highway 19 westward between Qui Nhon and An Khe. We carry a blivet, a 400-gallon rubber barrel of diesel fuel, to a column of five armored personnel carriers, APCs, on the highway. Ahead of us, a Huey approaches the armor column, and the last two armored personnel carriers stop to collect the Huey's load of C-rations and ammo.

The forward three APCs continue to a wider clearing and maneuver to form a protective circle to take delivery of our blivet of diesel fuel. The third armored carrier turns just past the point where the first machines left the road and pitches over onto its side, smoke pouring from its engine compartment.

Burrows grunts. "Land mine." We climb up to the base of the clouds and orbit above the armor column.

The first two armored personnel carriers open fire into the tall grass and tree line around their position while the last two armored vehicles hustle up the road to assist. The Huey flies over the crippled carrier, and the gunners open up on the tree line. We see no return fire.

"Hey, Windy Five, you're not leaving are you? We need that fuel." It's the lead armored vehicle.

"No, we're not leaving," I radio back.

"Who put you in charge, Mister Weatherill?" Burrows cuts in.

"Hey, Windy Five," Armor Lead starts, "we're running on fumes."

"When you're secure, we'll come in," Burrows answers.

The Huey lays a defensive perimeter over the armor column, while we hide under the clouds.

"You need Dustoff?" the Huey asks.

"We don't have time to wait for Dustoff. Come in here and get these guys," Armor Lead answers.

The armor column comes into view on my side of the aircraft. I see men lying on the ground, others attending their wounds. Personnel from the armor column are rigging a sling to upright the overturned carrier.

Without hesitation, the Huey banks to the center of the circle, lands and takes the injured men aboard. Then, the Huey comes to a hover, pedal turns toward Qui Nhon and departs to the east.

"We can take the fuel, now," Armor Lead calls.

"Are you declaring the area secure?" Burrows asks.

"No, I'm not, but I need fuel," Armor Lead answers.

One of our company Chinooks carrying a blivet of fuel flies alongside as we orbit over the armor column.

"Hey, Burrows, that you?" Company calls.

"It's not secure," Burrows answers.

"Looks secure to us." Company breaks off and begins an approach to the armor column. "We'll help these guys. You take your fuel on to An Khe."

"Roger that," Burrows says.

We leave the orbit and fly west to deliver our blivet to An Khe. We then shuttle fuel between Qui Nhon and An Khe all day. That evening we return to Phu Hiep.

"What gives, Burrows?" I ask. "They needed the fuel."

"If the place is not secure, I don't go in."

"This is a war zone. What does secure mean?"

"You just saw what it means."

I go to our showers and fail to scrub off the shame I feel, so I head to our little bar to attack it from the inside. Horton, Burrows and the other old-timers, gathered in their clique, don't give me the time of day. I get a scotch and lean against the bar. Another young warrant nurses his drink at a table. I go over to introduce myself.

"Antonio Alesti," he answers, and shakes my hand. His smile tips up the ends of his Clark Gable mustache. He's about six feet tall with olive skin. He reminds me of my Brooklyn cousins.

"Been here long?" I ask him.

"The bar or the country?"

"The 180th."

"Two months and two weeks," he says.

"Just a couple weeks for me."

"Let me guess, Weatherill, you flew with Burrows? You were in orbit over the armor column today. He made you feel less than honorable, I suspect."

"How do you know that?"

"Because his flying revolves around one condition: 'Is it secure?' Some guys love him, and some guys don't. I fall in with the latter. The way you keep looking his direction, it looks like you do, too."

"This is not what I signed up for." I swallow some scotch.

"He calls it 'irrational' if you jeopardize your ship. A lot to be said for that."

"But the guys on the ground?"

"We were passing by, so we helped the armor column. The Huey crew helped the armor column. We got him off the hook. We hung around and righted their injured APC. He wouldn't have done that, either."

"I wanted to bail out."

"That's one good reason we don't have parachutes; rotor blades are another. Next time, give him some shit.

Hell, give him a lot of shit. Instead of you trying not to fly with him, he'll find a way not to fly with you."

"Alesti, let me get you a drink." I get up and walk to the bar. I feel a grin working its way onto my face.

"If that's scotch in your glass," he calls over, "I think we like the same whiskey."

"It's scotch."

"Draw two."

*   *   *

Here at the 180th, I share a hooch with a guy named Loft. We room together but are members of different flight platoons. He's been in country three months. I heard that after his first flight his instructor pilot came into the company bar and whimpered through three martinis. After Loft's fifth flight, nobody will fly with him. Our commanding officer simply exiles Loft to Maintenance.

"Damn it, Loft! Why can't you keep your hands to yourself?" I'm looking at stuff that wasn't on my bed when I went out.

"All you do is bitch."

I unbutton my fatigue jacket and look around. "You rummage in my wall locker. You use my clothes without asking, you eat my food stash, and now I walk in and you're going through my footlocker. Damn it, man, this is my stuff. You can go to jail for this."

Loft holds a magazine from my footlocker in his hand. "I always put it back."

"That's not the point!"

I hear footsteps and someone pauses outside our door.

"Come in, damn it!"

The shadow moves on.

"Look, Loft, it's my stuff. I own it. It's mine. Most of it came from the States and has serious meaning to me."

"Sure, I understand."

My words just bounce off. "You touch my shit again... Aw, just forget it. Hands off, Loft, that's it, hands off!"

"You should see the doc. I think you're troubled."

"You trouble me. I listen to you talk in your sleep every night I'm here. I ought to record you. We'll see who's troubled. You've got some really strange requests."

Loft looks up from my magazine. "Bullshit."

I walk out into the central area and sit on a picnic table for a moment. The air feels good, cooling me down. I look for the shadowy stranger, but no one's around.

In the mail room, I run into Alesti. "I gotta get out of that hooch. That Loft is crazy."

"I heard."

"So, you like standing in shadows?"

"Screaming usually gets my attention." Alesti examines the cover of his new *Playboy* magazine, searching for the rabbit. "Why don't you just shoot him?"

"Hell, if I did that I'd be in Long Binh jail for the rest of my life. He just isn't worth that."

"Well then, move."

"Where to?" I ask.

"Didn't hear, huh?"

"No, what's going on?"

Alesti opens his magazine and unfolds the pinup. "Captain Thompson is leaving," he says.

"Your roommate? When?"

"About three days. Move in with me if you don't mind a hole in the wall."

"A hole?" I ask.

"Travis and I got a little drunk and cut a hole in the wall between our rooms. We don't have to go through two doors now. It seemed like a good idea at the time."

"Sounds practical. You just got yourself another roommate. Where's Thompson going?"

"South. He's wanted to transfer since his week in Vung Tau. He got married, you know?"

"Nope. Who to?"

"A Vietnamese national."

"Why would he get married? I've heard women are almost free in Vung Tau."

"I think he's Catholic," Alesti speculates.

My thoughts return to Alesti's offer. I really need to move. "You are serious?" I ask to make sure.

"Yep, something about out of wedlock. Besides, she's pretty."

"No, I mean about moving in with you."

His gaze leaves the centerfold. "I'm no prophet, Weatherill, but I think we'll do all right."

Three days later, we're drinking at Thompson's transfer party. We pour him onto a Herc around midnight for his flight south, and then we move all my junk to Alesti's.

3

Links to Home

Vietnam

A phone hangs on the wall in the breezeway that connects our hooches to the rest of the company area. It hangs there for one purpose only: to connect empty helicopters to the pilots who fly them. More than once, I walk past the phone and wish I could call home.

I'm waiting for the letters to start, the tape recordings to start. I feel like I've walked to the mail room enough to create a rut in the boardwalk. I write every day I can.

It took me almost a week to get to the 180th. It probably takes a week for my letters to get across the Pacific Ocean. Two weeks and a few days, America finally has my address. It will take a day for letters to start back, westward toward Vietnam. It might be another week before they find their way to our helicopter company mail room. Letters from home are due any day now.

One is here! An ink line to my home, my wife, my family; the envelope has a lipstick kiss on its back. I put the kiss to my lips and say thank you to the sky.

Back in my hooch, I read the letter a dozen times. My mind floods with thoughts of home. What do I write? I stand up and walk to the end of my bunk. What? I'm scared. I sit down and lean against the plywood wall. My thoughts spin like a globe of memory. I jump on and land in the front lawn of my father's house. In my hand is a stick attached to a string. The moon is out.

"Okay," my brother says, "my turn."

I hand him the kite tether as Dad comes out the front door. "When do you two plan to hit the sack?"

"We just passed four hours. I bet we're close to a record."

"A record, huh?"

"We'll probably be famous by morning."

My father looks into the night sky.

My brother sprints down the street. He can't keep tension on the kite. "I told you this was too much string," he yells.

I lose sight of the kite as it falls from the moonlight into the black above the roof.

Dad steps off the porch. "Wind quit?" His words follow the kite into the grass.

"Looks like it," I say.

My brother walks back as I roll up our sleeping bags. "What time did it crash?"

"Ten after."

"Not bad."

"Who do we write to see if it's a record?" I ask my brother.

"Guinness, I guess."

My dad looks at us. "Time for bed, worry about Guinness later."

Riverside, California: Annie

I'm almost finished with Jim's Christmas present, a calendar I've drawn on a strip of brown wrapping paper. The dates start at the top on November 20, 1967, the day he left for Vietnam. The months are stacked down the middle of the paper with November 1968 at the bottom for his return. Under the grids, I paint a branch that divides into two vines that twine up each side of the paper. As the vines pass through the seasons, I change the color of the leaves, and add snow to the bare winter branches.

The whole thing is about the size of a dish towel. The one consolation we have is that we can count down the days. I believe you can take just about anything if you know when it will end.

Vietnam

Captain Dodge, our platoon leader, is the son of a North Carolina tobacco farmer and holds a bachelor's degree in economics and another in history. It's a pleasure to fly with Dodge. He says what to expect and doesn't bust us for beginner mistakes. He teaches about war life; how the Worry Line—the crossing point into battle—draws itself across a person's path. Sometimes it's at the hooch door, sometimes at the operation briefing, and sometimes it's attached to bullets coming up from the jungle. It's a soldier's early warning system.

One day Dodge and our assistant platoon leader, Lieutenant Kase, call us together for a pep-talk. Kase is from Connecticut, still has a baby face, and comes from a family lineage that would not allow him to be a warrant officer. Dodge stands beside Kase, who sits on a picnic table. CW3 Horton and Burrows have pulled up lawn chairs beside Dodge. Dodge and Kase are halfway through their tours. Horton and Burrows are nearing the finish line.

"At ease, men," Dodge starts.

Alesti, John Travis, Al Styki and I sit comfortably on a couple of benches stuck in the sand in the middle of the U of the hooches. Travis is from New Mexico. Styki is an intense young man from New York. Alesti has been here the longest. Then comes Styki, then Travis. I'm still the new guy.

"It looks like the pipeline is drying up. We're not supposed to get any more pilots for a while," Dodge says.

"What else is new?" Styki pulls a pack of Marlboro cigarettes from his fatigue jacket.

Dodge gives Styki a "shut up" glance. "We're at fifty-nine percent manpower, and I don't see any changes coming. Huey companies can't get pilots, and Chinook companies can't get them either."

Styki lights his smoke. "What happened to the pipeline, Sir?"

"Beats me. All I know is we have pilots going stateside the next few months and no replacements in sight. Time off will become a premium. There's one thing else, and let me paraphrase." He takes a piece of paper out of his fatigue pocket. "Military etiquette has gotten a little lax. Just because this is Vietnam, the military has not changed."

"They're nuts, Captain," Styki blurts.

Dodge walks away without answering.

Kase gets off the picnic table and follows Dodge. Horton and Burrows already have evaporated.

Lieutenant Drum, Mister Loft, and Mister Morrow, members of our second platoon, stand in the breezeway of our hooches, listening.

Riverside, California: Annie

I open my eyes and untangle my feet from the covers. Reaching across my body, I help the little lump in my belly keep up with the rest of me as I roll from my left to my right side. The response is a tap dance on my bladder. I push up to a sitting position and swing my feet over the side of the bed.

An envelope has rested under my pillow for nearly two weeks. I obeyed the "Do Not Open Till Dec 20" warnings neatly printed on front and back, and I'm eager to see what's inside. I kiss the envelope, coax one end open and withdraw Jim's gift: a first-wedding-anniversary poem, renewing his vows.

-4-
Merry Christmas

Vietnam

We get our hair cut by a reformed VC lieutenant someone hooked with the name Lock and Load. His barbershop is in a shack that had once been our company tool shed. Because we live on the beach with sand as our yard, our commander saw no reason to keep mowers and trimmers, and has long since traded them for something else.

Lock and Load has four wives and a staircase of children who idolize him. His kids bring him gifts all day; tea, water, rice. His littlest daughter brings him bouquets of weeds and a coy smile. Watching the procession is like standing in a small stream that feeds a river.

One of our pilots, Tom Miller, has learned the language during his visits to the one-chair shop, and other places, and becomes our unofficial interpreter. He grew up on the family farm in Iowa, and loves learning new languages. He knows how to speak French and German, but no one else here speaks French or German. Army and Vietnamese are all that's left.

A few days after my twenty-second birthday, Lock and Load invites Miller and me to dinner at his home in Phu Hiep, between our compound and a beach of the South China Sea. The white stucco structure houses Lock and Load's third wife and two children. It's a three-room residence with beautiful, carved wood shutters instead of glass for windows.

Lock and Load greets us at the door and leads us into the main room where a low, circular table squats on a thick, round rug banded in bright colors. A mahogany plank bookcase stands against one wall, and the room is well lit by several hanging oil lamps. Sleeping mats and pillows are rolled up in two corners.

A boy and a girl show us to our places on the floor around the table, and then dash off. Lock and Load and his wife sit across from us. The children return with a tureen and pass our empty bowls as their mother scoops out our portions.

The main course is rice and vegetables mixed with other ingredients I don't recognize. My chopsticks capture a small, radish-like ball that unravels, unfolding a small, bare wing.

I look at Miller.

He picks up a ball and pops it in his mouth. "The baby bats are delicious, don't you think?"

I look at the bat dangling from my chopsticks. "Please tell them the meat is for the children," I plead.

"You'll insult them if you don't eat."

"Gifts aren't insults. Tell them."

"Chicken."

"Chicken, I'd be happy to eat. Tell them."

Miller relishes every bite and I vow to become a vegetarian for days afterward. Lock and Load seems polite on my next visit to his barber shop, just polite. I know I must redeem myself.

I decide to build a playground for the children of our Vietnamese workers. I get our commander's approval for the time it will take. I get everyone I can recruit to help. We trade and beg for leftover boards and pipe and chain; everything necessary to make a playground. We work at night, after our missions. Monkey bars, slide, swing, sandbox, are an instant hit.

On my second visit to one of Lock and Load's homes for dinner, his wife personally heats my can of ham and lima beans and serves them to me in the gold-edged bowl normally used by Lock and Load himself. After dinner Lock and Load offers to sell me his oldest daughter.

Lakewood, California: Annie

Yesterday, I drove Bonnie and a load of presents from Riverside to Lakewood, for Christmas at my parents' house. Gathered around the tree with me this morning are my parents, my sixteen-year-old sister Janice, and my sister Caty from college. A tape spins on Caty's tape recorder as we open our presents. I will add a personal message later before I box it up for Jim.

A jab below my ribcage startles me with the realization of how amazed Mary, mother of Jesus, must have been to feel the miracle of life growing inside her. I smile at the memory of Jim's reaction when he felt our baby move. I feel blessed and grateful for this precious moment of peace.

Happy birthday, Jesus, and Merry Christmas, Jim.

Vietnam

After we fly hot food out to the local firebases and outposts, Christmas shows up in Phu Hiep, South Vietnam: some singing and food cooked up special in our little bar; a few cups of happy whiskey; some presents from home to open.

Just as my mind succumbs to nostalgia, and my eyes rain, I power down a couple straight shots to sober up. Then I shoot a couple more to knock myself out.

Holiday euthanasia.

Merry Christmas.

Part 3

JANUARY 1968

325 DAYS TO GO

5

A Fine Line

Vietnam

The Capital Division of the Republic of Korea is based near Qui Nhon. A contingent of Tigers, as they are called, is moving through the mountains to the northwest of Qui Nhon toward Phu Cat, routing out Viet Cong regulars. With night and a rainstorm coming on, they've encamped on a ridge top. We have their supplies and some extra troops.

Sergeant Lee, our interpreter for the mission, sits in the companionway jump seat, plugged into the ship's communications. "Mister Horton," Lee begins, "there will be a small heliport on the north end of the ridge line."

"How small?" Horton asks.

"I do not know, Sir," Lee answers.

"Weatherill," Horton says, "tell them we're inbound."

"Tiger Ridge, Windy Four is inbound. Pop smoke, please," I say and look out the window

Yellow smoke drifts off a ridge about a kilometer to the northwest. It locates the heliport, and tells us the wind is almost calm. To our east we see pitch-black rain clouds push in from the South China Sea. In the west the sun begins to set.

"We've got yellow smoke," I acknowledge.

"Yellow, correct, Windy Four."

"It will take a moment to unload the men and supplies, Sir," Lee says in my direction.

I don't answer. Instead, I wait for Horton to respond.

"Okay," Horton says, "fast as they can."

"Yes, Sir." Lee nods. He unbuckles his seat belt and unplugs his headset to go aft to prepare his men to disembark.

Horton comes to a hover over the heliport, which is too small for the entire Chinook. He maneuvers and sets the rear wheels on the ground. The cockpit juts out over the canyon.

"Ramp going down," our crew chief calls on the intercom.

"Damn it, Chief, I'll call the ramp, not you," Horton scolds.

"Ramp coming up," our crew chief calls back.

Horton looks at me. "Keep your eyes peeled."

I open my window and look outside the aircraft.

"Ramp down!" Horton orders.

"Ramp going down, Sir."

With a flurry of activity the Korean troops disembark and begin to unload their supplies.

A cold draft slices through my window. A strong gust rocks the Chinook, and the helicopter's nose pitches up.

Horton immediately lowers the thrust lever (collective stick) at his left to decrease power and hold us on the heliport. To go down, push down. Pulling up adds power. Power is altitude: the more power, the more altitude.

At the same time Horton eases the cyclic stick between his legs slightly forward to lower the nose the foot it has risen. Cyclic stick forward, the nose pitches down; cyclic stick aft, the nose pitches up. Inches of control input will result in large movements of the helicopter.

When Horton moves the cyclic back to its center-neutral position, the shock absorbers on the rear wheel assemblies bottom out. Instantly, the helicopter jumps like a prodded animal. The violence of the buck locks my shoulder harness and pins me to the back of my seat. In three to five bounces the Chinook will self-destruct.

We only talk about ground resonance. We never do it in real training because of the terminal consequences— flying machine to hundreds of pieces of aluminum in four to eight seconds. At bounce three, a bang fires through the aircraft like a rifle report.

"Mister Horton!" the crew chief screams into his mike.

Horton is unresponsive to our eminent destruction.

A grinding noise floods the ship.

I pull the thrust up, and we leap into the sky. We are back in flight. The bucking stops and the rain begins.

"Mister Horton," the crew chief calls, "this bird is howling bad back here, Sir."

Horton does not acknowledge our crew chief. Instead, he looks at me. "Let go of the controls, Mister Weatherill."

I relinquish control of the aircraft. He is the aircraft commander and I am a crew member.

The metallic grinding and unnerving howl vibrate our bodies. The rain quivers on our windscreens.

"Mister Weatherill," someone keys over the intercom.

Horton turns our lives towards Qui Nhon. He flies at various speeds to try to moderate the howl and lessen the vibration. They do not abate. Neither does the rain.

"Mister Weatherill." My name comes back on the intercom. "Ramp up, Sir?"

A little flash, a transfer of loyalty and understanding, an oral handshake.

"Ramp up, Chief," I answer.

Our flight across twenty-one kilometers of sky, our return to the safety of Qui Nhon and Mother Earth, takes at least a year. Maybe it was a second, maybe twenty minutes. All I'm sure of is that it didn't take till the end of our lives.

We land in driving rain and Horton wants to taxi to some obscure ramp. I understand the fine line between duty and dereliction, but I also know there is a fine line between teamwork and tyranny. I reach to the throttle quadrant and pull the fuel levers, killing both engines at once.

Horton glares at me.

The howling abates.

"Thank you, Mister Weatherill," comes over the intercom.

The Chinook settles and hugs the earth.

"You're welcome," I answer. Then I light a cigarette and wait for hell to pay.

It doesn't take long. I'm called to Major Guilliam's office after we return to Phu Hiep and debrief.

"Mister Weatherill, your actions were aggressively insubordinate with Mister Horton," Guilliam, our operations officer, says.

"Sir, if I had not pulled the aircraft off the Korean heliport, the Chinook would have been destroyed."

"I doubt that," he answers. "Then, shutting down the engines at Qui Nhon. Who gave you the authority?"

"Sir, the aircraft was about to come apart. I had to do something."

"I doubt that, too. You seem to have an authority problem, Mister Weatherill. I want you to know I'm keeping my eye on you." Guilliam pushes his chair back from his desk. "You're dismissed!"

I've dreamed of flying all my life. My dad put me up with an instructor when I was fourteen. I was like a bear cub discovering honey, and I became an addict. I flew solo before I could drive alone. I still love the pungent mix of fuel and oil, the scent of wax and cleaners on the windows, seats and floors; the sound of the engine and the wind when the window is open in flight; the separation when the aircraft leaves the ground and climbs away from my planet and I can see the patterns on the earth below.

Here in Vietnam I'm in my element. In the cockpit I'm home in the job I have long dreamed of. I enjoy my business; it's the bullets and the bullshit I don't like.

6

A Low Profile

Riverside, California: Annie

The check arrives. Bills are due. Happy New Year. Today's mail brings a tape from Jim and our second military allotment check for $550. I deposit the check and transfer some money from my school fund account for school expenses. I also purchase a $50 money order for Jim.

Monthly bills to be paid are a $50.68 car payment and a $15 encyclopedia payment. Also due are one-time payments of $32 to register the car, $15 for Bonnie's obedience class, $4 for a dog license, and $86.50 for my college tuition.

I already paid $44.75 for books, and I'm not done yet. In addition to living expenses, I will replace a tire and use the patched one as a spare. Previously, I replaced the windshield wipers for $2.10 and had a tune-up for $15. Fred has pronounced my little red Datsun safe to drive.

Future major bills will be next quarter's tuition and books in March, baby supplies, and furniture before April, car insurance in June, and a trip to meet Jim in Hawaii for a week in July. Our parents have generously relieved us of food and lodging expenses.

*　　*　　*

I'm early and find a good parking spot near the humanities building at the University of California at

Riverside. It's my first day back after a year of married life with Jim as he completed flight school, and left for Vietnam.

All four classes are on Monday, Wednesday, and Friday. The first class starts at 8 a.m., and the last ends at noon. Tuesdays and Thursdays are free for study, housework, errands, doctor appointments, and whatever else pops up. The baby isn't due until a couple of weeks into the next quarter, so I figure I'm home free for now.

I gather four spiral notebooks and trudge up a slope to "Studies in Romanticism." In the classroom, I carefully slide into a seat and note the ample distance between the attached desk and my belly. I imagine next quarter, squeezing my late pregnancy body into the desk and needing someone to disassemble it to free me.

Over a ten-week period, I will read a combination of poetry and thirteen novels; write two, five-to-seven-page papers; participate in class discussions; and take a midterm and a final for this class.

Across campus, a visiting professor from Minnesota instructs my next class, "Deviant Behavior." He warns, "If you miss the midterm, there will be only one makeup exam. You must have a good excuse. Medical problems or confinement in any type of institution will qualify."

We also must read parts of two books and write an original research paper.

"Theories in Sociology" waits down the hall. We'll have the usual paper, a midterm, and final. We'll also slog cover-to-cover through a weighty textbook.

The fourth and final class is "Sociology of Confinement" with the visiting professor I met earlier. Field trips to prisons and similar institutions will cut into my Thursday time.

I'm a senior, but feel like a freshman in a new school. A few people look vaguely familiar, but that's it. I wonder which classmates also wait for someone to come home. I probably will not find out. The military advises families to keep a low profile. They tell us malicious pranksters have *called families to tell them a loved one has been killed or injured.*

According to news coverage, anti-war sentiment is growing, especially on college campuses. Reporters seem to salivate when cameras focus on demonstrations. They invariably refer to all protesters as students.

The effect is isolation of military families and denigration of students. I'm presumed to be both a potential fraud victim and a subversive. A low profile seems like a good idea.

Vietnam

"Mail call!"

"Huh?"

"Mail's here."

Mail? My eyes focus on the wall of the hooch wallpapered with my new posters of Bob Dylan and Humphrey Bogart, strange bedfellows in a strange place.

"Writing letters?" Alesti asks.

"Just thinking. Dreaming, I guess."

"I didn't mean to interrupt." He seems embarrassed; he knows my mind is not in Phu Hiep. "The mail's here."

"Thanks." I follow Alesti into the center court of our billets and up to a wood picnic table piled with letters and packages. It's my lucky day; two thick letters and a long tube-shaped package. I save the letters. The tube is from my brother. In it are reels of string, one for a Falcon, the other for a Captain America kite. I extract the kites gently from the tube. "I ever tell you my kite story?" I ask.

Alesti looks up from his letter. "I ever tell you about the Sylvestry twins?"

I don't answer. I let him finish his letter while I sit on a picnic table and read the note my brother stuffed in with the kites.

"Those sisters are incredible. They just don't let you quit," Alesti says.

"Sounds kinky." I look over my note and smile.

"Impressed, huh?" He grins back at me..

"Actually, I'm jealous." I fiddle with the Falcon kite, then return to the letter from my brother.

"I'd marry them both if I could."

"Just marry one and let them swap. How would anyone know?" I suggest.

"My mother would know and their mother would know."

"Your father would probably be proud."

"My father deserted us when I was three." Alesti tips his head.

"I'm sorry."

"It was long ago. I don't remember him. My mother doesn't even have a picture of him, anymore."

"How'd you wind up in Vietnam?"

"Nothing better to do, I guess. College was a washout. I started playing my guitar in some local clubs until they found out I wasn't twenty-one, then that washed out, too. The draft tried to get me. I couldn't see myself walking."

"Me, neither." We look at the letters in our hands.

"You're going be a daddy. How do you take it?"

"I love the idea. I didn't know I'd like it this much. But it's hard not being home with Annie."

"I couldn't take it," Alesti declares. "Nope. I love 'em and I leave."

"I remember special moments now. They help a lot."

"I make an exception for the Sylvestry twins."

"I think I would too."

7

Puppies and Fools

Vietnam

I'm in the shower, rinsing soap out of my hair, when Mister Morrow's .45-caliber pistol falls off his soap dish and lands on my foot.

"Morrow, damn you! Jeez, that hurts!"

"Oh, settle down. It's a good thing it hit your foot. It could of gone off if it hit the floor."

"You're crazy."

"Bullshit. If they came over the wire right now I'd be the only one with a gun."

"You moron! Our hooches are right there!" I put my head under the shower to rinse soap out of my eyes.

"Sure, cross an open field of fire. Go ahead."

I spit out some water. "First they have to cross the South China Sea to get to Phu Hiep. Then they have to cross the open area, then the mine field, then the guard towers, then the perimeter road just to get to your bare ass in the shower. Why would they want to do that Morrow? Just to get your sorry ass?"

"Because this is a fucking war, asshole."

I pick the .45 off the floor, release the keep and let the magazine slide out of the handle. I put it on the soap dish, then slide the breech open and lock it back. A cartridge pops out. "You shit." I walk down the line of showers, past Styki and Travis, and throw the .45, then the magazine, into one of the open commode holes.

Morrow stands behind me. "You'll regret that."

"Try me."

Neither of us moves. Finally, I get my towel and leave. Morrow rinses and follows. I stop in the doorway of my hooch to dry my hair. Morrow enters his hooch for a moment. Then, bending a hanger, he heads back to the commodes.

I write letters for an hour, waiting. I sleep with one eye open, my loaded pistol in its usual place beneath my pillow. In the morning, I drop my letters in the mail room and walk back to the hooches. Morrow is nowhere in sight.

I see Sergeant Steele and Corporal Jacaby on the boardwalk. Steele, a crew chief, reminds me of a tall, dark Paul Anka. He's from Michigan and has a brother in jail for car theft. Steele passed up street life for the Army. Like the rest of us, he's passing time marking off the days on his calendar until he'll be out of Vietnam. His brother is probably doing the same thing in a Michigan jail.

Jacaby, a frustrated chef from Ohio, usually flies as a gunner on Steele's ship. He'd been a company cook until he was caught with a gross of eggs in a Nha Trang whorehouse. His penance was a month in jail or a job as a helicopter door gunner. It turned out to be an easy choice.

"What's up, guys?" I ask.

"On a beer run, Sir. Come on, Jacaby," Steele says.

Travis joins me in the breezeway. "That was a pretty ballsy thing you did to Morrow," Travis says, shaking his head.

"I suppose so, but I didn't think of that at the time."

"I guess God does look after puppies and fools."

Riverside, California: Annie

Bonnie wriggles with excitement. I open the car door and she's in as if sucked up by a vacuum. She takes her place on the passenger seat and waits politely, but she can't contain her grin of pure joyful anticipation of going for a ride. She wears her new chain-link training collar. We've practiced every day for a week, and she's enjoyed the exercise and the attention. Tonight is her first official obedience class.

The class is on an asphalt basketball court. I attach Bonnie's leash and coax her out of the car. She rubs against my legs as we walk toward the court and stop near a group of about thirty people and dogs milling around. Bonnie puts a paw on my foot and presses her shoulder against my leg as we stand and watch. A poodle barks at a boxer, and a beagle across the way joins the chorus.

"Everybody!" The instructor's booming voice cuts through the turmoil. After a short welcome, he tells us to form a large square and face the center with our dogs. He explains that we will each be called to walk our dog across the square and back.

The boxer drags a stylish woman through the exercise. A teen-age boy with acne and junior high school sweatshirt does a nice job walking the family cocker spaniel as his mother wrings her hands on the sidelines.

We are next, and I start out. Bonnie reluctantly takes a few steps with me and freezes. I stop and look back to encourage her.

"Keep going," the instructor orders.

I tug Bonnie across the square and turn around. When she realizes we're going back, she trots along. When we retake our place, she hides behind me with her head between my legs as the rest of her classmates perform more or less successfully.

Back home, Bonnie insists I put her familiar leather collar on her. Then, she picks up one of my slippers, and we go to bed. She aligns her back with mine and sleeps straight through. When the alarm rings, she refuses to budge until I push her off of the bed and send her outside to relieve herself. When I let her in, she's bright-eyed. She accepts a treat and wags her tail.

8

Dishonorable Proposition and Tet

Vietnam

The breezeway phone rattles. After the third ring I walk over and pick up. "Weatherill," I answer.

"Sir, this is Corporal Garza, from operations. Major Guilliam said you're to meet him at the aircraft revetments. You're flying with him."

"Is this a Tac E?"

"Not that I know, Sir. But he wants you ASAP."

"Thanks. I'm on my way."

When I arrive, the aircraft's already running. My guess is a maintenance flight. I walk past two majors seated in the cargo compartment, and wave at the gunners and crew chief before I climb in the right seat and buckle up.

"It's about time you got here," Guilliam says.

"Where are we going, Sir?"

"You'll see."

Within twenty minutes we're flying low level orbits around a Korean outpost west of Phu Hiep.

"Are we landing, Sir?"

"We are not."

We hear the metallic tick of bullets hit the bottom of our Chinook. The door gunners fire at muzzle flashes in the jungle. After one more orbit, Guilliam turns on a heading back to Phu Hiep. He says nothing to us after we land; he simply walks away with the other majors.

The next morning Guilliam calls me to his office and hands me three citations to sign for Silver Star awards, one for him and the others for our two passengers. I refuse.

"Mister Weatherill, we discussed your insubordination before. How does a Flight Evaluation Board sound?"

"Actually, Sir, it sounds pretty good right now."

*   *   *

We are sent again northwest 200 kilometers from Phu Hiep to Pleiku. Our sister Chinook company, the Shrimpboats, is encamped a couple kilometers south of Pleiku Air Force Base at Army Camp Holloway. They have the misfortune of living in the middle of the Central Highlands. The countryside is beautiful, but the ground fire is too regular and deadly to suit any of us who officially reside on the coast.

At Camp Holloway, we live in a general purpose tent with cots for twenty pilots. Personal life ceases in this open volume of dreary space. No nightmare dream is concealed, no involuntary orgasm concealed, no scream against the absurdity concealed. We never ask where the scum on the shower floor comes from or what it is. Showering bare ass naked with boots on is not considered abnormal. And life continues.

Holloway, depending on the season, is either a mud hole or a dust bowl. In between seasons it's both. Holloway also has one of the best messes in the Central Highlands of Vietnam. The first time we eat there, we are impressed. By the third time, we start to see dirt in the corners, egg crust between the fork tines. We realize the flowers in the wall pots are imitations. Even so, we look forward to a great meal each time we pass through Holloway.

I run into some guys I know from flight school, once clean rogues, now red-dirt-covered rogues. We eat, and wind up looking for a drink in the gun platoon hooch.

The gun platoon lives in hooches altered somewhat in attempts to get a little privacy. The effect is a cross between carefree and paranoia. Some bunk areas are walled with lockers plastered with *Playboy* pinups. Next door, so to speak, is a bunk overlaid with sandbags on pieces of pierced steel planks. A plastic Jesus in one corner protects the mattress on the floor under the fortification.

"You hear what happened to Johns?" Bridger, a guy I enlisted with some eternity ago, asks.

"Nope." I swallow a shot of scotch, and light a cigar.

"Took a round in the thigh. If he wasn't hung on the left it would have taken his fun with it."

"When did this happen?"

"Two days ago. He's in Japan somewhere, now. They're building him new veins."

"What's Adams up to?"

"Who knows? He and Fraser never came back from Dak Pek. They had our best door gunners, too, those assholes."

"When was that?"

"This morning."

"Let's go look for them!"

"We already did. It's spooky; they just disappeared off the face of the earth. Never made it to Dak Pek, and never came back." Bridger swallows his scotch and pours another. "No marks in the trees. Just gone." He drinks again. The whiskey seems to have no effect on him. "Rumor has it that the NVA are massing along the Laos-Cambodia-Vietnam border."

I'm filling Bridger's glass when someone bangs on the hooch door.

"Everybody knows the damn door's open," Bridger yells. "Get your ass in here."

The door opens. A corporal walks up to our makeshift bar, looking thirsty and scared.

Boyd, Bridger's copilot, recognizes the corporal and pours him a whiskey. "Drink this, Brown."

"Thank you, Mister Boyd." Corporal Brown throws the whiskey into his mouth.

"What's up?" Boyd asks.

"Kontum. It's Kontum. It's under siege! Could I have another?"

Boyd pours. Brown gulps.

"Dak To, too. Everything that can fly is coming here for fuel and ordnance. The colonel wants everyone at the briefing room ASAP." Brown sets the empty glass down and vanishes.

It begins January 30, 1968, the Tong Cong Kich, the General Offensive: Tet. Soldiers die every day. Some die in the dark, some die in the light. What makes one day different from the next? All we know is that even more people are trying to kill us. Our history belongs to the future. We just want to make it to tomorrow.

The briefing is short and sweet. Hold American positions. Save American lives. We leave Holloway at 11 p.m., loaded externally with 6,000 pounds of ammo and half a pallet of C-rations for the troops at Kontum. Three Chinooks in and out, we make two trips from the logistics pad at Pleiku City and return so riddled with holes we're sent back to Holloway for repairs. Precious sleep, too, if we can keep our eyes closed.

Riverside, California: Annie

I thought going back to school would help me get through this year. But I was wrong. I feel suspended in time. I no sooner finish one assignment then go to another. It's all the same.

I think how little time I seem to have and how fast it's going, but when I look back, Jim's been gone only two months. We've really just begun.

PART 4

FEBRUARY 1968

294 DAYS TO GO

Night Flight

Vietnam

We've changed months, but it's only the next day. The attack on Kontum continues. In the morning, Chinooks move soldiers and ammo to defensive positions around Pleiku. In the late afternoon, our Chinook goes back to Kontum with food, ammo and water. At the east end of the airfield, we see five tanks backed into one another to form a star. Enemy dead surround the tanks.

The tank commander comes on the air. "We need machine gun barrels next time you come. Is that clear?"

"Yes, barrels."

Short and to the point. They get their barrels on the next sortie. Then, our aircraft is pulled off the resupply.

Captain Dodge is outside the aircraft, getting briefed on our next mission by two majors who arrived in a Jeep. I supervise the refueling and preflight. We all know another long flight period is coming and we need our bird in top notch condition.

We're eating our C-ration dinner when Dodge comes to the rear of the Chinook. He stops and looks at the sky. The day holds only a few more hours of sunlight. "It figures," he mutters, coming aboard the helicopter.

"What figures, Sir?" I ask.

"The weather." He comes up and sits on the bank of nylon seats opposite me. Our crew chief hands him an open, warm can of spaghetti and meatballs.

"Thanks, Chief," Dodge says. After a few bites, he looks up. "This is what we're up to. Some folks need to get to the Special Forces Camp near Dak Pek. Sending a bunch of Hueys will probably cost a crew. So, we're going in right at dusk, alone. We can get everybody in at once." Dodge pauses and eats another couple spoons of spaghetti. "Any questions?"

"Fuel?" our crew chief asks.

"Just what the tanks will carry. We're going to have to make it round trip from here."

"Suggestion, then, Sir," our crew chief continues.

Dodge nods. "Go ahead."

"Load up, start up, and leave with fuel caps dripping."

"Do it, Chief."

I climb in the cockpit, open my plastic map and put my finger on our present location. Just in front of my fingernail, my Worry Line crosses the chart. I measure out our flight path between a finger and thumb.

Dodge enters the cockpit. "What's it look like?"

"Well, Sir, as a bird flies, about 130 kilometers. Over the highways and in the middle of the valleys, about 150. An hour's flight each way. No headwinds, best estimate. I'm afraid the short way will take us over too many enemy gun barrels."

"That leaves us fifteen minutes of fuel for problems."

"Problems will be our undoing, Sir."

Dodge looks out the companionway to the rest of our crew. "You men hear that?"

"Yes, Sir," they answer in unison.

"Questions?"

"Fifteen minutes can disappear pretty damn fast, Sir," French, the left door gunner says.

"Amen," Dodge agrees.

Our human cargo has arrived. They load up and get comfortable. Their leader comes to the cockpit and introduces himself.

Dodge goes aft to brief our passengers. "When we land at Dak Pek we'll need you off the helicopter in record time. We'll be very thin on fuel. Frankly, gentlemen, any delay could cost all of us our lives. Thank you for your attention. We'll have you there in about an hour," he says and comes forward.

"We're starting, Chief."

"Clear aft, Sir."

"Clear left. Clear right," French and Jacaby, our door gunners add.

After we start, ground handlers top us off and replace our fuel caps.

"Fuel caps secure, Sir," our crew chief says, climbing aboard. "Ramp up, Sir?"

"Ramp up, Chief," Dodge says.

And we're off.

"You were looking at the sky earlier, Sir," I say.

"A little late for the weather isn't it?" Dodge looks over with one eyebrow raised.

"Just a little chit chat. I can tell rain's coming. It may help us hide," I say.

"You always seem to see a bright side to things."

"Thank you, Sir. Only, sometimes the bright side is just making it to the end."

"Like now?" Dodge asks.

"Yes, Sir, like now."

We fly north. As the valley shadows grow longer, we fly on the sun/shadow line using the dark to hide and the light to see the deadly ridges alongside. We have our position lights turned off and talk to no one outside our helicopter.

As we pass Kontum, we pick up a few tracer lines, but no bullets hit our craft or rotor blades. We hear battle conversations and calls for supplies. We recognize friendly voices all around us.

"Where's that Chinook going?"

"They talking to anybody?"

We proceed, cautious of our fuel flow. *How do you make a helicopter burning four gallons a minute sip fuel?* According to my map, we are one-third of the way to our destination, Dak Pek. Increasing clouds overhead soak up the sun, blotting out any chance of using a star or two to detect drift.

Captain Dodge looks at me. "Comments, Mister Weatherill?"

"Sir, we're losing daylight too quickly. We're going to need some guidance to land." We know that if we use a homing tone, the NVA will realize that something's up. If we miss Dak Pek Special Forces Camp at the end of our dead reckoning, we'll need to turn back immediately.

"There's Dak To, Sir," French says from the left gun port. Oil lamps in the village glimmer yellow in the twilight.

"Thank you," I answer. We are two-thirds of the way.

"Well, they're supposed to light a couple 55-gallon drums." Dodge says.

"We'll have to be on top of them to see any light from the bottom of a drum."

"Time, heading, speed and distance, the basic tenets of aviation. Everything else costs extra," Dodge comments.

"Okay, Sir, heading 300 degrees for fourteen kilometers. Time, six minutes; then, heading 005 degrees for fifty-two kilometers. Time, nineteen minutes. Time is started."

After six minutes, Dodge turns to 005 degrees. We have climbed to 700 feet above the ground—all the altitude the cloud bases will allow us.

"Time's up," Dodge says. "We should be there."

Dak Pek is not under us. I restart the clock. One minute. Two minutes. We are traveling at two kilometers per minute.

"Sir, we need to turn around."

Dodge has begun the turn just ahead of my words.

Minute four and we are now headed south.

"Fly this thing, Weatherill. I'm looking for the lights."

"I have the aircraft, Sir." I hold heading, altitude and airspeed.

Our door gunners see the lights first. "One o'clock low," French calls. "You got them, Sir?"

"Lighted drums in sight," Dodge acknowledges. "I have the aircraft."

"You have the aircraft, Sir." I, too, see the barrel glow through the chin bubble.

"I'm on the approach," Dodge announces. "Give me airspeed, rate of descent and altitude, please."

"Speed, 100 knots; descent, 500 feet per minute; 600 feet above the ground," I say.

"Thank you."

"Speed, 70; descent, 400 feet per minute; 400 feet above the ground," I continue.

"Okay," Dodge affirms.

"Speed, 50; descent, 300 feet per minute; 300 feet above the ground."

"Good, I've got a good view. Follow along with me."

I put my hands and feet on the controls without applying any pressure. I will take control if something should happen to the flying pilot.

"Sir, there's a crashed plane, right side low!" Jacaby calls.

I look out my side window. We're descending beside the wreckage of a Caribou cargo plane.

"How we look?" Dodge asks.

"Plenty of room," I say. "Clear right."

He completes the approach and we land.

"Ramp down. Everyone out!" our crew chief yells.

And we wait.

It takes less than two minutes to clear our twenty-four passengers and their gear. "Everyone is out. Ramp is clear," our crew chief calls.

"We're leaving; ramp up, Chief," Dodge says.

"Ramp coming up, Sir."

We climb straight up to the base of the clouds and follow the reverse of our inbound headings, distances and times. More than half of our fuel is spent, and it has started to rain.

"Okay, everybody," Dodge starts, "we're headed home. Keep a sharp lookout. We're going back the way we came. And men, no shooting. Our tracers will give us away."

The intercom comes alive with double clicks, the "no words, I understand" signal.

The sound of our helicopter has awakened the enemy. Tracer lines search for our sound signature.

"You know, these guys might shoot each other across this valley," Dodge jokes.

I want a cigarette, but I'm not going to present a light to the darkness. Then, we are past the tracers.

"Dak To, Sir, port side in the distance," French says.

We make our first turn. The rain has become a drizzle. We cross our five minutes of easting and turn south. I see, or imagine, a glow on the horizon. Kontum is still fighting back.

After landing at Holloway with, we think, seven minutes of fuel in our tanks, we all have a chance to breathe. We meet in the interior of our Chinook, shake hands and head to the transient hooches.

"You passed, Mister Weatherill," Dodge says.

"Sir, I enjoy your company, too."

Against the Odds

Vietnam

We mark time on handmade calendars from home, the work of mothers or children or wives. We stare at the squares of months and weeks and days, and drift in and out of sanity. Our memory is in control of days gone, and our fate in control of days ahead. The calendar is love and hate, fear and happiness, blatantly obvious in meaning and harshly secretive. It's okay to look at someone's calendar, but not to make comments concerning it, unless invited.

I have to be in Phu Hiep to cross off the days on Annie's calendar. When I'm gone for a week or more, crossing out the days is pure joy. If I've lost a friend, it's full of despair. Everyone I know occasionally sits transfixed, optically welded to his calendar; sometimes nodding his head, sometimes moving his lips. When I walk in on Lieutenant Kase, he's doing both in the middle of the night. His chin is so low it almost bounces off his chest. I've just been awakened to fly, and we are scheduled to fly together.

"You okay, Lieutenant?"

He throws a letter and photos on his bed. "Look."

I pick up the pictures. "Who's the naked lady?"

"My wife."

"Hmmm." This doesn't bode well for the beginning of a tactical emergency mission. "Who's the naked guy?"

"Our neighbor."

"You a nudist, Sir?"

Kase's chin falls back toward his chest. "I've been writing her a letter."

"I'm sorry; I didn't mean to be a jerk."

"Hey, I'm sorry I missed the fun. What do you want, Weatherill?"

"Tac E. You and me. Two other crews."

"Be right with you."

"You sure?"

"Three crews sounds big. I don't want to miss the excitement."

"See you at the briefing, then."

War for Chinook pilots is mostly resupply and waiting to get shot. We fly resupply all day and hang around our hooches all night, waiting for something to happen. Normally something bad happens every few days. To mete out the bad evenly, we have our Tac E List. A tactical emergency means somebody is getting hit and running out of people or ammo; the critical stuff.

Huey crews fly tactical emergencies, too, but when the loads are large, the Chinook crews get the call. One Chinook equals about three Huey loads. Huey or Chinook, we can always count on Huey gunships—well armed guardian angels—showing up during the mission. The weather has to be impossible to penetrate for them not to show.

The worst missions are black, rainy night tactical emergencies. We get called out of bed, and time blurs until we lift off the heliport. While the rotor blades hack away at the night, we sit in the cockpit, strapped in a seat, and chain smoke. Now time crawls. Tactical emergencies are the devil's lottery; some are easy to win, and others pay out in death.

Major Guilliam, a pilot on tonight's Tac E List, is in charge of the briefing. On the flight assignment board are the names of the three crews, but Guilliam's name isn't among them. Everybody sits down and we get our frequencies, coordinates and the intelligence report with the salient features of the mission. Tonight the mission is to move three loads of troops from a southern landing zone to a northern landing zone. The catch is, the northern LZ is under siege.

Every pilot on the mission takes furtive glances between the names on the crew board and the Tac E List. There's tension like a low-grade fever. Helicopters are assigned, and we set our watches. The briefing is adjourned. The helicopter commanders order their copilots out to preflight the machines, but nobody moves. It's time to do something about that fever.

CW3 Peters, the ranking warrant of the night's pilots, steps forward and addresses Major Guilliam. "Sir, you aren't going with us tonight?"

"No, Mister Peters."

"Would you tell us why?"

"Mister Peters, your crew is waiting."

"Sir, with due respect, we all have to accept the Tac E List and the even-handedness it represents. People are even a little superstitious about trading places on the damn thing. We've never taken anyone off the list before, although we have made trades. The list makes a little part of this crazy war fair."

Peters has given Guilliam a graceful way out. He must have made a trade, but with whom?

As Peters speaks, our platoon leader, Captain Dodge, comes through the door. "Looks like I'm right on time," he says, shifting the weight of his body armor across his shoulders.

It appears that the trade was with Dodge, because of his hasty appearance in the briefing room.

"Captain Dodge, this is none of your affair," Guilliam snaps, throwing his clipboard on a desk.

Well, so much for a trade.

"You're not telling us something," Peters continues.

"You're on report, Mister Peters. All of you out!" Guilliam orders.

No one leaves. In dice rolls with fate, the list is the only equalizer.

Dodge runs his fingers through his sweaty hair. "I went by battalion. LZ Tara is fighting a large force of Viet Cong. We won't have any high air cover at the LZ. Cloud ceilings are way too low. We might not even see any gunships. The whole coast is socked in with fog and rain. The weather is moving south pretty fast. If we don't get up there tonight, LZ Tara will be overrun."

Peters stands nose to nose with Guilliam. "Bastard!"

Guilliam smiles back and leans toward Peters' ear. "Fifty percent survival rate," he whispers. "I look forward to seeing you again, Mister Peters."

I grab Peters by the elbow as he prepares to swing and pull him toward the door.

"I'm flying with Peters," Dodge says calmly. "Miller, get lost."

Peters nods. "It's up to you, Captain." He shakes his head at Guilliam. "It's a fair trade."

Miller looks around. "Anyone want to stay?"

There are no takers.

Dodge glares at Guilliam. "We'll all be back, Sir."

And we leave: Kase and I, Alesti and Styki, Peters and Dodge. Miller stands outside the briefing room as we walk by. His body armor leans against his leg, and the light of the bare bulb outside the door reflects off his dejected face.

Three Chinook helicopters head for a firebase carved into a ridge of the coast range. We land one at a time and fill with men we are to move north to LZ Tara. We're heavy and barely hover.

Kase and I slide off the ridge through the only cut in the trees, and a downdraft drops us onto the firebase's antennae farm. Thin aluminum poles bend and scrape along our belly. Clinging to flight with our engines at maximum power, we drag ourselves into the night.

"Get on the radio," Kase says. "Have them stay with the trees. The cut's a downdraft."

I key the radio. "Ten, this is Eight."

"Ten," Dodge responds.

"The cut's a downdraft. Stay with the timber. You'll be heavy."

"Thanks," Dodge answers. "Nine?"

"We heard." It's Styki's voice. "Looks like the clouds are lowering, too."

We pull our loads off, one by one, descending at maximum power into the coastal canyon, looking for flying speed. We turn for the South China Sea and then north up the coast to Qui Nhon, our refueling stop. The rain has started, along with wind and turbulence and lowering ceilings. We have eighteen soldiers on board, plus our two gunners, two pilots, and crew chief.

Ammo boxes, a couple bazookas, a mortar tube and each man's pack fill the ship's center. Under the shrill scream of the Chinook's engines and transmissions, many sleep, oblivious to the noise tearing at their ears. Qui Nhon appears out of the rain thirty minutes later, and we land.

The wind is 30 knots gusting to 45, and the ceiling north is low. It's 1:50 a.m. and the rain is warm. We fill our fuel tanks while those soldiers who can't sleep mill around, chain smoking in the rain.

We pilots gather on the aft ramp of Alesti and Styki's Chinook and go over our predicament with nature and our burdened helicopters. The fact that our destination is under siege is pushed into second place.

Kase looks at me, and a broad smile comes to his lips. "I don't have any problem going first."

"Why not?" I shrug in agreement. "Put your money where your mouth is," I mutter under my breath.

Peters motions the grunt officers over, and we huddle around a hand-drawn map of LZ Tara. The heliport is on the west side. Randomly strewn Xs locate enemy gun positions.

"This is what we've got. No guarantees any of this is current," the grunt officer points out.

The head grunt frowns through the water dripping off his ragged battle helmet and inhales deeply on the unfiltered cigarette cupped in his hand. "This fucking place." His cigarette smoke comes out in short bursts with his words and drowns in the wet night. "Wake everybody up. It's time for a talk," he orders.

A lieutenant and some sergeants standing next to him disappear into the dark.

In minutes, fifty-three soldiers, most naked from the waist up except for their dog tags and helmets, stand quietly in the warm night rain, waiting for number fifty-four to speak.

The captain stands in the dim light illuminating the ramp of the Chinook. "The fight has started without us. When you run out the back of your bird, this is where you go." He holds up the map, pointing out the plan for the insertion, and then looks around. "Gentlemen, if you have any questions, now's the time to speak up. This is not going to be easy."

The only sounds from the group are cigarette coughs.

"We all know people at LZ Tara. They're counting on us. Don't forget your buddy. Remember your job." Fifty-four hands his lieutenant the map, lights another cigarette, and heads for our ship.

Everyone disperses, and the only sounds are rain and sloshing footsteps.

A grunt breaks the silence. "Shit, I was just starting to unwind, man."

A couple people laugh.

Kase joins me trying to stay dry under the back of our Chinook. "At least the rain's warm," he observes.

"I suppose," I answer.

"My wife's always been an exhibitionist. Clothes were never a big thing with her," Kase continues.

Men pass us, loading through the back ramp.

"I sort of got that impression, Lieutenant."

"I didn't tell her to stay home and knit, ya know."

"It's your life." I say. "It's not my call."

A soldier who's been smoking behind me finishes his cigarette, crushes it under his boot and looks at Kase. "You want to trade problems tonight, Sir?"

Kase tosses his smoke into the night behind us. His cigarette hisses and dies in a puddle of water that has probably come all the way from the Philippines. "Pretty short notice," he answers, as we climb into the back of the Chinook.

"Does that mean no, Sir?" the grunt asks.

I look at him. He's maybe nineteen, but looks deceive. I follow Kase toward the cockpit.

"I guess it does," Kase mutters.

We load our helicopters and start our engines. It's my turn to fly.

"Qui Nhon tower, Windy flight of three ready for takeoff. We require the runway," Kase says into his boom mike. "All set, Weatherill?"

I take a deep breath and exhale. Thin streaks of old smoke come out my nose. "Yes, Lieutenant, I am."

"Steele, Jacaby, Rodriguez; you ready?"

"Yes, Sir, Lieutenant," Steele responds for all three.

"Windy flight is cleared for takeoff at pilot's discretion. Wind 200 degrees at 27 knots gusting to 40. Altimeter 29.62. God speed, gentlemen."

"Cleared for takeoff. Thank you, Qui Nhon."

We taxi into position on the runway and pull in maximum power. The Chinook trembles and accelerates forward on its tires. It's nice to have a runway to get our helicopter into the air. With the cyclic stick pushed forward our rear tires lift first, cleaning the air to the aft rotor head. The gusting wind, pushing our helicopter around during the takeoff roll, eventually produces flight.

The end of the runway rushes past, and we are catapulted into the night above the bay of Qui Nhon. The only reference points to use against the turbulence of the storm, the rain, and the dark, are the instruments on our panels. We might as well have been shot off an aircraft carrier somewhere on the South China Sea.

"Three hundred feet is as high as we can get. Our blades are in the clouds," Kase keys over the tower frequency. "Lots of rain. How's your instrument work, Nine?"

"This isn't the Sahara," Alesti answers.

"Ten?"

"Thanks, Eight, we got it," Peters responds.

"Gab, gab, gab. You'd think this was Armed Forces radio," Styki transmits through a cigarette.

We fly east, straight offshore to get around a hilly peninsula on our left. Then, we turn north and follow the coast, praying we'll be able to see any landmass before we run into it. We've managed to climb to 600 feet.

The rain is unrelenting, and the wind pitches us about. The black of night and sea and rain and clouds consume us. If we crash into the sea, we'll be swallowed faster than a fly gulped by a frog. We fly on with our side windows cracked open to let our cigarette smoke escape.

"Ten, Nine." Alesti's voice breaks the radio silence.

"Go ahead, Nine," Peters answers.

"How many minutes out you make us?"

"Fifteenish,"

"Yeah, that's what we figure, too. Only problem is number one engine. Oil's heating up and the pressure's dropping."

"Stay with it, Nine." Peters encourages.

"We figure on melting it rather than shutting it down."

"If it's any comfort it looks normal from here," Peters offers, flying in trail of Alesti and Styki.

"Thanks, Ten."

Kase and I exchange glances. That's all it takes for complete understanding. I go back to my instruments, and he goes back to looking at the rain, the black night, and the South China Sea. Other than the sea, the only place to land is in the middle of a siege.

Our crew chief, Steele, hears the conversation. "I'm worried about them."

Kase twists toward Steele. "We'll all be fine."

As we move northward along the coast, the mountains beside us drop to a river valley, and we see the light show at LZ Tara through the rain.

Steele looks out the windshield from his position in the companionway. "When I volunteered for maintenance, they didn't tell me a crew chief had to do this stuff."

"They lie a lot," Kase offers. Some of his blond hair, wet with sweat, hangs out of his helmet.

Steele keys his intercom. "Hey, Jac, you ready?"

"Let's rock and roll," Jacoby responds.

Steele looks at me. "You know it's Rodriguez's first trip?"

"First Tac E?"

"No, his first trip. French is grounded by toe rot. He could barely walk to the dispensary. He saw the doc and got grounded." Steele looks toward the gunner. "Rodriguez is a virgin."

Rodriguez stamps his feet to let us know he's listening.

"A virgin?" Kase says.

"Wrong sex, sorry." I grin.

"I'm watching him close," Steele assures us without using the intercom and leaves the cockpit.

As Steele passes, Rodriguez rolls up the sleeves of his fatigue jacket, showing his barracks tattoos—1968 living art.

We turn west up the river valley and fly into instantaneous war. Thirty-seven millimeter air bursts erupt like black umbrellas opening in the night. Tracer fire punches red streaks up into the sky. Three big, noisy Chinooks draw attention, but this is too much gunfire, and too quick. Clouds, rain, fog, this is the only way we could come, and they knew it.

"Hang on!" I yell. I roll the helicopter toward the center of the valley, and dive toward the trees. We skim the tops as fast as we can go. Jacaby, Rodriguez, and several grunts open fire out the left and right gun ports.

"Yeah, motherfucker, yeah!" Jacaby screams.

"Don't melt your barrels, boys," Steele yells. "Take short bursts!"

In the back, we hear bullets hitting the Chinook. Someone screams.

"A grunt's hit," Steele calls up.

I look at Kase. "Now we know why Guilliam was grinning from ear to ear. Let the VC have us!"

More metallic clicks and Kase lifts his feet off the floor. "Shit!" A bullet smashes against the armored bottom of his seat and clanks to the floor.

A scream comes from the left gunner's position. Rodriguez, hit in the leg, writhes on the helicopter floor. A grunt grabs Rodriguez' machine gun and continues firing.

Steele fires the M79 grenade launcher from the back of the Chinook. "How much longer?" he shouts into the intercom.

"A couple more minutes," Kase says. "Who's helping Rodriguez?"

"A medic and a grunt," Steele pants.

The two men are on Rodriguez, compressing his wound and stabbing morphine into his pain.

As we close in on Tara, the ground fire intensifies. I roll the Chinook left and right, hoping to avoid the bullets. A streak of tracers punches through the blades, and the blades begin to whistle. The ride is suddenly dry. The rain has stopped.

We land next to three armored personnel carriers parked as a shield. Our forward blades are so close to the front carrier that a bullet couldn't squeeze through. Another minute and we are empty.

"Clear!" Steele screams, and raises the ramp as we start our departure.

"Heads up!" Kase yells.

We jump into the night, turn over the top of LZ Tara, and flee to the coast. Jacaby and the new grunt door gunner wade in shell casings. Once again, the helicopter cannot go any faster.

Nine lands in our wake. We are a third of the distance to the sea when Nine is out. Then, Ten lands. Ten is out.

Rain envelopes us and a wall of tracers awaits between LZ Tara and the coast. Water on the windscreen blurs the tracer lines. Jacaby and our new gunner fire continuously.

"Easy on those barrels!" Steele yells, while comforting Rodriguez.

Normally, our Chinooks would be loaded with wounded, but even the soldiers at LZ Tara don't think we can make it out. None of us has lights on. Separated by only a couple minutes, we no longer see each other. Radio contact is all we have.

"Lieutenant, tell them we're going into the clouds," I tell Kase.

Kase is barely visible in the glow of our instruments. "Eight is going into the clouds." He announces.

"Nine is going up," Alesti reports.

"Ten is going up. Punch your clocks. Fly 090 degrees for ten minute," Peters says.

"Nine, copy."

"Eight, copies," Kase affirms.

Tracers are everywhere. The clouds around us radiate an eerie dim glow.

"Hey, Ten," Alesti's voice is strained. "Number one engine just quit. We're still flying east."

"Okay, Nine. Listen, it was five minutes from the coast to Tara. Let down when you get to six minutes. Do it easy and glue yourself to the altimeter. Don't go lower than 500 feet," Peters instructs.

"Yes, Sir," Nine replies.

"Eight, copies. We'll tell you where the bottom is," Kase breaks in.

We begin our descent at six minutes. The clouds go dark as though someone has flipped a switch. The tracer wall retreats behind us.

Kase reads out the altitude, "One thousand ... 900 ... 800 ... 700 ... 600 ..."

We drop out of the clouds and slow down to allow the others to catch up. Then, at ten minutes, we start a slow turn south for Qui Nhon. The bullet-less blackness eases the tension.

"Lieutenant, turn on the lights so Nine will have a reference," I say.

Kase radios back to Nine and Ten. "Clear below 600. Let us know when you see our lights."

It doesn't take long. Nine, with Alesti and Styki, joins up. Peters and Dodge bring Ten out of the clouds and turn in trail with us. It's a long forty minutes to Qui Nhon. It probably seems like days for Alesti and Styki flying through ink on one engine.

We land in Qui Nhon and leave the broken helicopter and our wounded behind. Alesti, Styki, and their crew ride with Peters and Dodge.

We return to Phu Hiep with the rising sun. Dodge wakes our commanding officer to let him know we're home, and to lodge our complaint about Major Guilliam's conduct. A group of six pilots standing outside the C.O.'s hooch gets his attention.

"What's up Dodge? I see you're all back safe." The C.O. looks us over. "Congratulations, gentlemen."

"Thank you, Sir. Sir, where's Major Guilliam?"

"Nha Trang."

"You sent him away?"

"I didn't send him away. Battalion called with an early resupply and Major Guilliam and Lieutenant Drum took it out. It's our business, Dodge. What's wrong?"

"Sir, he was supposed to be on the mission last night and took himself off."

"Do you know why?"

"Fifty percent survival estimate."

The C.O. mulls over Guilliam's action and says, "I'll handle it. You men get some rest. We move a White Horse firebase at noon."

So we go to bed. It's a dreamless and very quick sleep.

Riverside, California: Annie

I wish I could pray for Jim, but I know somebody will die and someone else will grieve. I can't be so selfish to wish that on anyone. This is the hardest thing I've ever done. My selfish prayer must be that God will not give me a burden that I cannot bear. If He chooses to grant my prayer, Jim will be safe.

Is my faith strong enough? Just to hedge a bet, I put in a request for a guardian angel to be assigned to Jim, if God has any spares handy. I hope He doesn't mind.

Every night Janie burns a votive candle in the bathroom. The candle and a Saint Christopher's medal on a chain sit on a ceramic dish. I appreciate her prayers for her brother's safety. The flame seems to give assurance that all is well.

The candle also serves as a night light for the times our growing baby uses my bladder as a springboard. Tonight, I get up and grope my way down the hall. As I touch the bathroom door, it swings inward. The draft blows out the candle. The darkness grabs my heart.

11

Problems, Promotions, Practical Jokes

Vietnam

The Korean White Horse Division is encamped in the coast range south of our base at Phu Hiep. They pushed the Viet Cong back into the coast range and are going after them with a firebase. We're moving the old base twenty kilometers west to an area full of VC supply trails. The plan is to have the base up and firing as quickly as possible.

"Keep it coming down, slower, hold position," Steele directs. "Stay with me."

Miller flies while I monitor our instruments and scan the tree line on my side of the cockpit. As we hover, our rotor wash hits the ground at 90 miles an hour and puts up a dust cloud that resembles a small nuclear explosion.

"Hooked!" Steele calls.

"Aul krear," Korean ground radio informs.

"Let's go up, Sir," Steele urges.

And we come up slinging a 105 mm howitzer and a piggyback of ammo off the ground. We have the last of the cannons to be moved. Racing against nightfall, the firebase sights its guns while its flanking mortar platoons take sporadic small arms fire. We're low on fuel and eager to have the day over.

Lieutenant Kase and Mister Morrow, ahead of us, finish placing a cannon as we turn up the ridge line for the firebase.

Kase's voice comes on the radio. "We're coming out."

"We're on the ridge east, right behind you," Miller answers.

Steele is on the floor of the Chinook, peering down the cargo hook hole. "Below us! Running on the trail! Must be twenty of them!" he yells.

"Who?" French asks. Gauze hangs from his unlaced boots.

"Your foot rot go to your head; just who do you think?" Jacaby puts them in his sights and opens fire. "VC!" he screams.

"Where? Where?" French hangs out the left gun port to the end of his harness.

"We're right by them." Jacaby fires another burst.

We relay the sighting to the firebase.

Kase keys up. "You guys okay?"

"Not sure," I answer.

We hover over the vacant gun position and Steele starts talking. "Down three, that's good, ammo's on the ground. Down ten."

Miller lowers.

"Left five. Easy, easy. Stop. Hold there. Hold there." We come to a hover above the cannon. "Down. Gun's five off, four, three, two, shit, ow, damn ow, ow, one."

"We're taking fire!" French yells.

"Talk to us, Steele," I cut through. We hear bullets hitting us.

"Down one. Down one! Okay, release. Release!"

"I did," Miller acknowledges.

"No release! No release! Hold position." Steele reaches into the hook well and pulls the manual release handle. "Steady!"

"Hey, Boss, we've got a hydraulic shower started back here," French calls, "coming from the center of the overhead."

"Steady, dammit!" Steele scolds.

An explosion rocks the helicopter. I scan the instrument panel. The number two hydraulic pressure is zero. The number two engine fire warning comes on bright red, and the ring of the fire bell floods the cockpit.

"You're clear!" Steele yells. "Clear! Clear!"

Jacaby cuts in, "Hey, number two's on fire!"

"French, clear us left," I call.

"Yes, Sir, clear left," French calls. "Damn, there's nobody to kill," he adds.

"I'm landing," Miller says. "Let's get out of this thing."

Steele comes on unknowingly. "Ow! Damn, ow! Shit."

"What's going on? You got smoke pouring from number two!" Kase yells over the air-net frequency.

"Somebody help Steele! Let's go!" Miller calls.

"I'm unplugging," Jacaby says, and we hear him run aft to help Steele.

Miller lands on the firebase. "At least we're among friends," he says.

I pull the number two fire handle and shoot both extinguisher bottles into the engine. We work to shut the helicopter down. "Do Koreans drink scotch?"

"We're going to find out," Miller replies.

"Hey, shit for brains." It's Morrow's voice.

I don't answer. I finish the emergency checklist.

"I hope you have a fucked night, asshole. I can see them all around the firebase. I just thought you'd like to know," Morrow concludes.

Below the nose of the Chinook, Korean soldiers work with the industry of ants, putting up a sandbag wall.

Miller reaches up and turns off the master switch. The helicopter goes dead. "Let's get out of here," he says.

"I'm right behind you," I answer.

The Koreans haul Steele out the back of the ship.

A sergeant gives some orders in Korean, and then looks at us. "Please, Sirs, you follow me. Your men will be very well." He dashes off with Miller and me at his heels.

We follow the sergeant down a sandbagged staircase into a plank-lined room. A Korean corporal appears after a moment and leads us through a door at the back of the room. We descend another flight of stairs and enter a long tunnel lit with bulbs overhead in wire cages. Along the floor, mines are wired into the wall. It feels like we're in a dusty submarine set to blow itself up. The corporal opens a door to a room with two beds, lockers, and a small table near one wall. Two privates bring pitchers of water, bowls, soap and towels. Miller and I wash up.

"Maybe they'll have scotch," Miller says, wiping his face.

"This much civilization is a pretty good sign," I say.

The corporal reappears, and leads us to a small dining room where he introduces us to the commander of the firebase. The commander sits at the head of a table large enough to seat eight. On a desk next to him is a map of the firebase and the surrounding trails. Behind him hangs a larger version of the map. At each side of the commander stands a private. We communicate through an interpreter.

As the evening progresses, the attack reaches the firebase. The commander dispatches privates with orders for the surface, and they return with information. He moves pieces similar to chessmen around on his map while we eat.

The Koreans serve us a four-course dinner. The food is delicious, though many of the odors and forms are unrecognizable to my Western nose and palate. After dinner, we return to the bedroom and sleep. If the firebase commander has any scotch, he hasn't made it available.

The next morning, we ride out on a resupply bird that arrives behind a couple Dustoffs picking up wounded. We leave our Chinook behind for maintenance.

"Miller, I need some information," I begin.

"Sure."

"If I write an endorsement for an award, who gets it?"

"Lieutenant Drum is our awards officer. He passes them on to Major Guilliam."

"Do I pass it by Captain Dodge?"

"You don't have to, but it's the right thing."

I nod my head. "Good, thank you."

"Just so you know, Dodge is putting you up for aircraft commander," Miller says. "He told me they want you and Travis promoted within the week. The standards instructor is coming through to flight check both of you on the 28th. If you don't want this now, now is the time to decline. The wheels are turning. Dodge is determined."

"Congratulations Mister Weatherill," Steele says.

"Congratulations, Sir," Jacaby and French put in.

"Thank you, gentlemen."

The week flies by. Travis and I take our oral exams about the workings of the Chinook helicopter, mission planning, and emergency checklists. We fly in the traffic pattern of the Phu Hiep Airfield, demonstrating our ability to handle engine failures and emergency landings. We pass our exams for aircraft commander and have drinks in our officers' club in the midst of handshakes and slaps on the back.

CW3 Burrows approaches us at the bar. "You two have your work cut out for you," he says. "Nice you made it." Then he walks away.

"Wow," Travis says. "Is that an inroad?" he asks.

"I think it is." I drink my scotch and order us two more. "You given any consideration to a call sign?"

"I have," Travis starts. "I'm from New Mexico. New Mexico was the 47th state to join the union. Windy Four Seven, what better?"

"Well done."

"How about you?"

"I looked at the history of our unit. Alphabetically, I'm the 70th officer. I'm going with Seven Zero."

"Seven Zero, nice touch."

It's late afternoon, the scotch has settled me, and it's time for a nap. Heading for our hooch, I meet CW3 Peters in our open area.

"Congratulations, Mister Weatherill," he offers. "I was just going to operations. Glad I caught you."

"Thank you, Sir."

"Just keep your wits about you. Hold your emotions until you get out of the cockpit. I've found the two don't sit together well."

"Yes, Sir." I nod in acceptance.

Peters shakes my hand and walks away.

A couple hours later, Travis wakes me and hands me a glass of scotch. He's tipsy and sits on the end of my cot. "You're not going to believe this."

"Believe what?"

"I was coming around the corner from the bar and heard Dodge and Peters talking in Peters' hooch."

"Eavesdropper."

"No, wait. Dodge is furious. Peters was at the operations room today, checking on something. He stepped outside for a smoke." Travis drinks some scotch.

"And?"

"He heard Lieutenant Drum and Major Guilliam talking about valor citations that Peters submitted to Drum. Guilliam said he's not sending them on because warrants and enlisted don't deserve high awards."

"What!"

"True is true." Travis lights a cigarette.

"Who were they for?"

"I don't know. I don't want to know."

*   *   *

Travis and I lie in the shade of our bird parked in the grass alongside the runway at Nha Trang. We've come for some Huey pilots and a load of enlisted men. The C-130 Hercules bringing the men from Tan Son Nhut is late. We don't mind lying in the soft, thick grass, but we're due out for other resupply, and now we're getting behind.

The Hercules finally lands with our load of new folks. We finish our smokes as the group of twenty passengers arrives at our Chinook. The men bend from the weight of their duffel bags and the long hours of travel to get this far in country. They flop down in two disheveled rows alongside the helicopter. Their tired eyes have cannon-fodder glaze.

A wiry lieutenant bounces over to us.

"Hello," I say.

"You forgot the 'Sir,' Mister."

"Who are you?"

"Lieutenant Parson. I'm ranking here. If you're finished lying around wasting time, I'll get my men on board. Who's in command of the helicopter?"

"You're looking at him."

"Then I suggest you get your ass in gear."

"Okay, let's go. Load 'em up, Chief." I walk to the back of the Chinook and climb on board.

"Who's the shithead?" Steele asks under his breath. Thanks to the Korean medic, his arm healed nicely and he's back at work.

"Who knows?"

Lieutenant Parson marches the group of warrant pilots and enlisted men onto the ship and comes forward to the cockpit. "Let's get this show on the road."

I climb out of my seat and grab the lieutenant by the front of his shirt, lifting him onto his toes. "This is my ship. On my ship I'm in command. If I hear one more word out of you, I'll have you thrown out of this helicopter while we're in flight. Do we understand one another, Lieutenant?"

"You can't do this."

"Trust me."

I let go of him and return to my seat. We start our ship and leave Nha Trang eastward over the South China Sea.

"Hey, Weatherill, do you feel like messing with the lieutenant's head?" Travis asks.

"Sure, how?"

"How about a quick trip over the free-fire zone for a little practice?"

"Great idea."

"Hey, Steele, you hearing this?" Travis asks.

"Yes, Sir."

"Pass the word to everybody but the asshole. This should be fun," Travis says.

"Done, Sir."

We climb to 1,000 feet and level off directly over a small, abandoned village on an island a couple miles off the coast. I reach the overhead panel and turn on the red alarm light and bell. At the same instant, the gunners fire their machine guns and Steele pumps rounds out the grenade launcher.

All the briefed passengers duck in their seats. A couple pranksters yell, "We're hit!"

The lieutenant bolts to the cockpit. "We're going down, you incompetent shit!" he shouts above the noise. "When we get on the ground, as the highest ranking officer on board, you can be sure that I will assume command immediately."

"Didn't you get the word, huh?" I ask, trying to look innocent.

"What?"

"The word, Sir," I repeat.

"What do you mean?" he asks through gritted teeth.

"This is a free-fire zone. This was just a preparedness drill."

"You'll hear more about this, Mister."

"Some people just never get the word, I guess," Travis says and shrugs his shoulders.

These are our first flights as aircraft commanders in Vietnam. Travis flew to Nha Trang and I flew back to Phu Hiep. I'm thinking it went well.

After two other sorties, we land, debrief, and are released for the day. It's 2 p.m.; we pop open a couple beers and sit at a picnic table. CW3 Horton drags a footlocker out of his hooch. Then, he goes back in and reappears with a duffel bag.

"Well, look at this. Mister Horton's leaving today," Travis says. "I'd completely forgotten he was this close to going home."

Horton comes up to us. "You see any papasans?"

"Nope," Travis answers.

"Great," Horton starts. "This man's Army is going straight to hell. I can't wait to get back to some sanity."

Travis and I watch Horton work himself up.

"What are you two doing?"

"Drinking beer," Travis answers. "We're lamenting that this is a leap year. Everybody gets an extra day of war."

"Not me," Horton says. "Somebody else can have the bad luck. I'm leaving."

"Mister Travis and I have been upgraded to aircraft commander."

"Well, I guess that was bound to happen. Too soon, I think."

"You want a goodbye beer, Mister Horton?" I offer.

"Hell, no."

I look at Travis. "It was a genuine offer."

Travis smiles. "So was his response."

"Well, grab these things and take them over to the road," Horton orders.

Travis cocks his head to the side and whispers, "What do you think?"

"I think he hasn't said any of the magic words," I whisper back.

We swallow more beer. I take out my cigarettes and offer one to Travis. He takes it and we both light up.

"Get this stuff over to the road. The Jeep should be here any time," Horton urges.

"We won't have to do anything else for him," I suggest under my breath."

"Okay," Travis agrees.

"What the fuck are you two talking about? Horton shakes his head. "This is the problem with the Army today, no respect. I ought to get a flame thrower and stick it up both your asses."

The Jeep arrives and the corporal climbs out. He grabs Horton's footlocker and finds it too heavy to lift.

Travis hops off the picnic bench, takes one end of the footlocker and helps the corporal move Horton's belongings. I drag the duffel bag. Horton follows.

"Thank you, Mister Travis," the corporal says.

"Sure," Travis answers.

I toss the duffel in beside the footlocker.

"Thank you Mister Weatherill," the corporal adds.

"Take the rest of the day off," I suggest.

"I'll tell them you said it was okay."

Horton climbs in the passenger seat. "Let's go; I've got a plane to catch.

PART 5
MARCH 1968
265 DAYS TO GO

12

A Little Recreation

Vietnam

Alesti has used his time in country creatively. He knows his way around and has a proclivity for procuring things. He's quiet and discrete. I've watched Alesti leave on suspicious missions long enough. I drop hints and he takes me into his confidence. Under his wing, and after introductions with his contacts, I, too, am accepted.

One morning, our commander sends us to get some party goodies for about sixty people. Alesti and I know some of those attending will be important guests because he hints that battalion is involved. For a makeshift refrigerator, we pull up the forward floor panel of our Chinook. We fill the cavity with crushed ice from the mess hall, then replace the floor panel.

We fly south to the central logistics pad at Cam Ranh Bay to take delivery of the items we need. When we land after our sixty-five-minute flight, we learn that our main cargo, our cover for the trip, will be delayed for two hours. A fuel truck arrives and tops off our tanks.

Door gunners Jacaby and French, crew chief Steele, Alesti, and I sit on the dusty, but cool, floor of our Chinook, smoking cigarettes and shooting the breeze until the heat around our heads gets to us. At the side of the logistics pad is a runway for airplanes, and beside that is a small, sandy beach behind a concertina wire barrier.

"Suppose we can go for a swim?" Alesti asks.

"Beats me." I shrug.

"What about the wire, Sir?" Steele asks. "Maybe there's a path the locals use to get through."

Steele and Alesti pull their cool butts off the floor panels and walk out the back of the helicopter into the heat. Jacaby and French follow.

"I'll watch," I announce.

"Do that, you lazy shit," Alesti says.

Sitting on the floor, I lean back against the web seats along the side of the cargo compartment. I pull my daily, hand-rolled Italian cigar out of my pocket, nip off the end and light up. The cigar is from the box my uncle sent from New York. They're the same brand he smoked when he was a tank commander in World War II. The taste is sweet, the nicotine thick. I climb out of the Chinook and watch the crew poke around the wire.

"Come on, over here," Alesti calls, standing by the route Steele discovered through the wire.

I knock the hot end off my cigar and follow.

After about an hour of swimming, sunning, and more swimming, the five of us float around, telling all the jokes we know. Three men appear at the concertina wire. They follow our trail and stop by our piles of clothes.

One man sifts through the fatigue jackets. He picks one up and calls out, reading off the front of the shirt, "Mister Weatherill!"

Steele covers his eyes from the glare off the water. "The man's a colonel, Sir."

The colonel calls my name again. "Mister Weatherill, front and center!"

I slosh out of the warm water. "Yes, Sir, how can I help you?" I ask, standing at naked attention.

"Mister Weatherill, this area is off limits," the colonel starts. "And what are officers doing swimming with enlisted men?"

I remember something my father told me, something about any offense is better than your tail between your legs. "A little relaxation, Sir."

The colonel looks at his companions and my gaze follow his. I realize that instead of one colonel, there are two, and the man in the middle is a general. This definition of Worry Line was left out of my training.

The general folds his arms. "Is that your helicopter on the pad?"

"Yes, Sir."

"It's unsecured."

"With respect, Sir, that would make the entire log facility unsecured."

The second colonel's lips tighten. "You're out of order, Mister!"

"With respect, Sir," I repeat. My Worry Line wraps itself around my legs and climbs toward my neck.

The general turns to leave. "We'll see you at your aircraft. Five minutes."

"Yes, Sir." I wait a moment as they walk away. "Come on, we're going to have a meeting!" I call to the others.

We dress and retrace our route through the wire to the helicopter. We stand on the sunny side of the bird to let the warm sun dry our hair. Cigarettes come out, and I re-light my cigar.

The general and his two colonels pace in a conference huddle about twenty yards away. Suddenly, the first colonel bolts our way.

"Put out those cigarettes!" he roars.

We throw our smokes on the pierced steel planks of the runway.

"Stand at attention. This crew is a disgrace. Consider yourselves on report."

Alesti steps out of line. "Sir, we arrived here on schedule for our load. We've been waiting for hours. The cool water is the only relaxation we've been near in weeks."

Bulging veins appear on the colonel's forehead. "I'll tell you when you can speak!"

The general and his aide return to the colonel's side to glare at us.

"Misters, follow us," the general's aide addresses Alesti and me. The three men walk away, shaking their heads.

Alesti turns to me. "This could be interesting," he mutters.

"Define interesting."

"Dinner in the Long Binh jail."

We follow the general and the two colonels beside the runway. We have no doubt we eventually will go to jail. While we walk, a Jeep pulls up.

"General, your plane has called for permission to land," the man informs, and drives away.

They stop, and Alesti and I come to attention.

"You men are setting a poor example," the aide begins. He glances at the general and then back at us. "There is a separation that must be maintained, especially where color and rank are concerned. It looks very bad."

Alesti comes out of attention. His expression has an iciness that surpasses the colonel's. He walks directly to the general. "Sir, that soldier, Sergeant Steele, saved my life last week. With all respect, Sir, I didn't realize you maintained a racist on your staff." Alesti glares at the general's aide.

The general, his face drained of color, stares at Alesti. "You and your partner can be in a very inhospitable jail for dinner tonight if you don't disappear."

We come to attention, salute, and vanish. We return to the helicopter and hide in its shadow. Then we light up.

The whine of turbine engines drifts from the cloudless sky as a procession of loaders pulls up to our helicopter with our supplies. Alesti stands to inspect the manifest.

While cargo is loaded, the twin engine plane coming for the general and his colonels enters the traffic pattern. It turns base leg, and then final approach.

"Hey, Alesti, watch this!" I call.

Alesti comes into the sun from the rear of the Chinook.

I run to the side of the runway, frantically waving my arms above my head as the plane rushes by for its landing. The pilot in the left seat waves with an arrogant flip of his wrist and touches down with his landing gear up. The propellers of the U-21 cut into the pierced steel planks of the runway. The pilot jerks the plane back into the air and lowers the landing gear. The gear lowers halfway down before the aircraft runs out of flying speed on bent propellers and settles back to earth, grinding to a stop in front of the general.

"At least they kept it in the center of the runway," Alesti compliments as we watch the crew slink out of the airplane into the teeth of the colonels.

Steele walks up. "Time to go, but I think we're too heavy to hover, Sir. We got everything we came for."

I ride to the scene of the crash on a loader, jump off, and sort of stand in the way until I get the general's attention. "Sir, our helicopter is loaded. We can leave, but we're too heavy to hover. We need the runway."

The general glares at me with murder in his eyes.

"Sir, while the loader is still available we can unload the helicopter and sling the U-21 out of the way."

The general passes me without uttering a word and proceeds to the loader. He points to his U-21. "Move it!"

The loader operator drives onto the runway, spears the fuselage and proceeds to push the basically undamaged airplane into the sand. When the loader pulls back to free its forks, the plane doesn't slide off. The loader operator bangs the forks up and down, cracking the aircraft fuselage behind the wings, and finally pulls free. Then, he drives into the logistics complex, whistling to himself.

I return to our helicopter and we leave. The loading delay, the heat and the runway problem with the general's plane have reduced the ice on the lobster and the T-bone steaks to cold water. We unload a pallet of supplies at the last firebase on our sortie sheet and fly home. The mess sergeant meets us on our company heliport and dashes the food to his own form of emergency room.

As we walk to the operations room to debrief, a corporal runs toward us. "Hey, the old-man is on the phone, and whatever he's discussing involves you. He wants to see the whole crew."

We know we're dead. The five of us walk into our colonel's office, and stand at attention. We think we look pretty good, considering the day's dirt.

The C.O. puts his phone down. "The meat made it okay. That was the mess sergeant."

I clear my throat in success toward Alesti.

"Not so fast, Mister Weatherill." The C.O. shakes his head at me and then turns his attention to Alesti. "About your insubordination. That pisses me off! Did you really imply racism in the general's command, Mister Alesti?"

"Yes, Sir, I think it was the heat," Alesti says.

"You were asking for it. And you, Steele, you have a good swim?"

Steele stands, thinking about an answer.

"We even tried to wave off the fixed wing," I chime in.

"Yeah, that was good. But let's face it; you guys can get under people's skin real fast. Take a break. Three months, that's all I've got left. Go easy on me. Now, get ready for the party."

We all salute and leave his office.

"What'd the general say?" Steele asks.

"The general's staff doesn't like officers swimming with enlisted crew members." Alesti picks up his body armor and helmet.

"The hell they don't," French says with a smile forming on his face.

"You got in his shit, huh?" Steele continues.

"I got as far in as I could without Mister Weatherill and me going to the Long Binh jail for dinner."

"Thank you, Mister Alesti. Mister Weatherill."

"I'm ready for some party time," Jacaby says and walks away. French follows, walking to his own beat.

Alesti and I dump our flight gear at the hooch, pour two long scotches, and hit the showers. Refreshed, we walk to the party and work our way through the crowd to sit where the bar meets a side wall. Steele and Jacaby are helping as bartenders.

Steele leans across the bar. "Sarge figured the T-bones medium-rare. Both want stuffed potato with the lobster."

"He's a mind reader," Alesti compliments.

Our commander walks up to us. "The general wants to meet the parties responsible for the fabulous food."

We follow him to our grateful guest.

"Sir, I'd like to introduce Mister Alesti and Mister Weatherill. I believe you gentlemen have already met."

The general stands and gently pushes the C.O. aside. "Yes, we've met."

No one ever told us who the guest of honor was and we never asked.

"We're all here to help, Sir," I say, shaking the general's hand. Alesti and I retreat to our corner to hide.

As we finish our meals, the general approaches and taps Alesti on the shoulder. "Thanks for trying to save my plane, Mister," he says, then shakes Alesti's hand.

"It wasn't me, Sir," Alesti says looking my way. "It was Mister Weatherill. I know we Italians all look alike."

"Well, thank you then, son."

We shake on it.

13

All in a Day's Work

Vietnam

Miller and I are in flight, headed to the Nha Trang log pad. He's returned from R&R in Hawaii.

"What was it like?" I ask. "I'm going there when I get my time in."

"It was fabulous. We just walked and talked. We wanted to go simple, but damn, it went so fast!" he bemoans. "It seemed so long in coming."

"Windy Twelve, we've got a couple blivets of diesel for you. All we have left are long slings. Any problem with that?" the log pad radio operator asks.

"Shit," Miller says, "I really *am* back here!"

"Any problem with the slings?" I ask him.

"No."

"Log Pad, long slings are fine," I tell them.

"Okay, Sir, two blivets to go. Twelve o'clock, a hundred meters."

"You ready, Chief?" Miller asks.

"Yes, Sir," our crew chief responds.

We hook onto our load and shudder through translational lift; the transition from hover to flight. The blivets are for two locations: an American armor column and a Korean firebase. We head west from the Nha Trang log pad.

The day is pleasant, with no storms nearby, and only a thin, broken layer of white clouds near the blue water of the coast. The gunners listen to Armed Forces Radio, and we go over the other sorties for today. Many times, we can combine drops and save a trip, like the log pad has just done for us with the blivets.

After about twenty minutes, we approach our first drop rendezvous. Since I'm not flying, I do the radio work. "Armor Six, this is Windy Twelve."

"Windy Twelve," Armor Six answers, "there may be a delay."

"Geez, that sounds like gunfire, lots of gunfire," Miller says.

"Armor Six," I call. "How can we help?"

"Windy Twelve, we're taking mortar and bazooka fire. We think the attack is coordinated from the farm house in the center of the clearing in front of us, over."

His transmission crackles with rifle reports.

We fly around a ridge and a bend in the highway and see the fight. The propellant trail from a bazooka begins in a pit beside a white stucco building. The armored vehicle targeted by the bazooka lurches backward to avoid the rocket, and the gunner in the vehicle's turret opens fire with a .50-caliber machine gun.

A mortar tube pokes out of a camouflaged trench behind the farm house, which protects the mortar position from frontal attack by the armor column.

"They need gunships," I say.

"Get them. Get on it!" Miller says.

I change from the FM radio to the UHF radio. "Nha Trang Control, Windy Twelve, over."

"Windy Twelve, Nha Trang Control. Go ahead, Sir."

"We need immediate gunship support. Coordinates follow." I relay the coordinates to Nha Trang and give them the ground situation. Miller has put us in an orbit behind a ridge for protection, but we still see the fighting. If we orbit too long, the VC will move assets to try to destroy us, too.

"Windy Twelve, Nha Trang."

"Windy Twelve," we respond.

"We have gunships in your area. ETA five minutes."

I pass the information to the armor column.

The column spreads out, making it harder for a mortar round to land on the carriers. Their .50-caliber machine guns keep the bazookas at bay. The gunships close in and call Armor Six for a situation update. When they finish, I inform the gunships of our location, and Miller maneuvers out of harm's way. The gun team rolls in on the mortar position and salvos rockets and 20 mm cannon fire into the trench. The mortar fire ceases.

The armor column moves off the road and approaches the farm house. About fifty meters from the house it stops and waits for the gunships to attack. After five or six rocket hits, a large secondary explosion collapses the house. The helicopter gun team comes around again and fires on the bazooka pits, producing small secondary explosions.

"Nice shooting," Armor Six calls. Three armored vehicles drive to the farmhouse and blast it with .50-caliber machine gun fire.

The gun team breaks off to position for another attack. Gun Lead keys up, "Do you need anything else, Armor Six?"

"Can you stay with us while we get our diesel blivet from Windy Twelve?"

"Affirmative, Armor Six."

Two other armored vehicles rake the tree line with machine gun fire.

"Gun Two, you copy?" Gun Lead asks.

"Two copies."

The armor column ceases fire and forms a circle. We land the blivets, and release their diesel supply. Then we come straight up, and begin our journey to the Korean firebase.

"Windy Twelve, Armor Six, thank you for the coordination."

"Our pleasure. We'll be through here all day. Call if we can be of further assistance," we say.

"Roger. Armor Six out."

"Well, that was an interesting start for the day," I offer.

"Sure was."

"Fuel's getting low, too."

"Real quick at the Koreans, then," Miller says.

We fly in and out of the firebase with no delays and turn back to Nha Trang and more fuel.

Riverside, California: Annie

Bonnie has found her niche as chief caretaker. I had a private chuckle when the obedience instructor told our class we would spend more time with our dogs. At home, Bonnie looks after me as if I were a child. Promptly at 9:30 each evening, she sits in front of me and declares it's bedtime. "Mrrff," she announces. She doesn't want to hear about papers due or tests the next day. "Mmmuh," she insists, with her chin on my knee. She knows what's best and will not give up until, finally, I go to bed.

Sometimes, I continue to study while sitting up in bed, my expanding girth serving as a book rest. Once I stretch out on my side, Bonnie jumps up and aligns her back against mine for the support I need to sleep.

Sleep slips in when exhaustion opens the door and withdraws when pummeled by tiny fists and feet. The match continues till near dawn, when the baby curls up into a solid, immovable ball, and sleep rushes in.

When the alarm clock goes off, Bonnie gives me fifteen minutes to get going. Meanwhile, she waits outside the master bedroom door until Fred comes out, gives her a belly rub and lets her go outside. If I've not made sufficient progress when she returns to check on me, she jumps on the bed and licks my ears. No matter how our day goes, Bonnie does her best to make sure Fred and I start on time and with a smile.

14

A Brief Taste of Freedom

Vietnam

It's a wear-your-civvies days, T-shirt and cutoffs warm. Alesti and I take turns trying to get the Falcon kite in the air. The Captain America goes straight up, like turning a pigeon loose. The Falcon kite is obstinate.

"Maybe it needs more tail. It dips too much," I say.

Alesti throws me his handkerchief. I rip it into long, thin strips and tie some together.

"Maybe I should take the Captain and you take the Falcon," Alesti suggests.

"I like a little challenge. You're on."

I hold the Falcon above my head and run. Each stride jerks at the kite, urging it to climb. And climb it does. In about five minutes it's tethered at the end of 100 feet of line next to the Captain America. All it needed was a piece of tail.

"Not bad," Alesti compliments, opening the first two cans of our six-pack.

"Was there ever any doubt?"

"Not the least. I heard you and Travis got in some trouble, something about scaring a new guy."

"We had to see the colonel."

"What'd he say?" Alesti asks.

"Don't do it again. What'd you expect him to say?"

"That you were grounded a couple days."

"No such luck. As short-handed as we are, I don't

think there's any way you could get grounded no matter how hard you tried."

Lieutenant Kase comes past the end of the hooches onto the perimeter road that separates us from the gun towers and two concertina walls that border Phu Hiep. "How about a couple more feet of line?" he asks, tossing each of us another roll of string.

"Thanks, these things could wind up in orbit," Alesti says and takes a sip of his beer.

Kase helps me add an extra roll to the Falcon and then helps Alesti set up the Captain. "It'll cost you boys a beer."

"Fair enough." Alesti punches a can open with the "church key" opener and hands it to Kase.

Kase gets comfortable in the warm sand between us. "I got more pictures of my wife. These are better. She's with another girl and a few guys." He digs inside his shirt and pulls out an envelope full of pictures. "Here, look for yourselves." He hands the stack to me.

"Look, it's none of my business." I hand the photos to Alesti.

He immediately lays them out on the sand. "Pretty good stuff."

"Thanks," Kase replies.

"What are you doing?" I ask, looking at the pictures upside down.

Kase turns a couple around. "It's okay. She wrote me a long letter explaining why she's doing this."

"Why is she doing this?" Alesti asks.

"They're in her art class and right now they're drawing nudes."

Alesti picks up one of the photographs and puts it close to his face in scrutiny. "Damn, look at this one. These guys look like they have three legs." He tosses the picture over to me.

I glance at the picture. "What else did she say?"

"She's sending me divorce papers."

Alesti scrutinizes a few more photographs, then picks

them all up, stacks them and puts them back in the envelope.

The extra string is just what we need. The kites rise like weather balloons. They fly magnificently, and the beer goes fast.

Children from Phu Hiep appear on the other side of the concertina wire walls and launch their own homemade kites. One box kite takes three children to fly. Other kites are various shapes and sizes colored red, blue, yellow, and green. Some tails are elaborately embroidered dragons. The children's laughter floats in the air.

I can't help but smile.

Kase puts the envelope back in his shirt. "I think if I find a virgin I'll be okay."

"You need to meet the Sylvestry twins." Alesti says, finishing his beer.

"No, just a virgin."

"Why?" I ask, getting to my feet to give Kase the tether to the Falcon.

"Because I need to start all over from scratch."

"Virginity has nothing to do with it," Alesti insists. "What you need is a woman. Take the divorce and let me find you one."

Our kites float back and forth over the concertina wire and the mine field between us and Phu Hiep. The afternoon peace seems out of place.

I leave to get more beer. On the way to our small officers' club, I see Morrow carry his body armor out of his hooch. I stop to avoid a confrontation. He walks through the breezeway and out of sight toward the operations building.

Morrow's door opens again, and his hooch maid appears. Her hair is wet and matted, her face bruised. A thin red line trickles from the corner of her mouth to her chin.

I walk over and hand her a piece of the torn handkerchief. She keeps her eyes down.

"I'm sorry," I say.

She glances at me and flees into Lock and Load's barber shop.

I go to the club for more beer, then return to Alesti and Kase.

"Hey, Lieutenant," I say to Kase, "Morrow's maid just came out of his hooch with a cut on her face. I watched Morrow leave, and then she came out."

Alesti takes the six-pack out of my hand and passes back a can.

"This is bullshit. We need to do something," I say.

Kase nods. "I've already discussed Morrow with the C.O. Your shower incident traveled fast. So did his comments to you and Miller at the Korean firebase."

While we discuss the problem, a captain pulls up in a Jeep. The "OD" cuff on his upper arm tells us he's the airfield officer of the day. He climbs out of the Jeep and marches over.

"Having fun?" the captain asks.

"Sure are, Sir," Kase answers.

"Well, the fun's over, gentlemen."

Alesti pulls a new beer out of the six-pack. "Oh."

"We've had two complaints in the traffic pattern. Those damn kites are a hazard."

"We were just going to roll them in," I say.

"I'll save you the trouble." The captain pulls a knife from the sheath hanging from his belt.

"What's the big idea?" I ask, too late.

The knife blade cuts the two tethers, severing the land links and the memory links and our freedom links, in the blink of an eye. The Falcon goes into a high-speed spin and lands on the perimeter road fifty feet in front of us. The Captain America swoops in big, lazy sways before it pitches up and then dives straight down. It accelerates as it falls, finally stabbing into the sand between the concertina walls. I shake my head. *How in the hell will I get my kite out of a minefield?*

The children from Phu Hiep quickly reel in their kites and scamper back to the village.

The officer of the day climbs back in his Jeep and races, with the engine roaring in first gear, to the Falcon. The tires crush the fragile sticks and rip the lightweight plastic fabric. Then he backs up to the three of us. "I want your names."

We look at each other and shrug our shoulders. I walk away from his demands and threats and retrieve the broken remains of the Falcon. Then, I add that captain to my mental get-even list. There are others to keep him company, but I have yet to get even with anyone. I don't see myself as a badass. Yet, for what little bit of ego I possess, I have decided to keep adding people until I actually get even with someone.

The Captain America kite becomes a landmark between the concertina walls along the perimeter road. I tape the Falcon to the ceiling of our hooch. It brings back memories each time I look up at it.

15

Nightmares and Firepower

Vietnam

A chant, "vet nom, vet nom," accompanies a bass drum. People stand around me. Someone adds a new language to my blood chit. Someone offers $20,000 for my life. I cannot see the faces.

Rainy night, headed for a spot on my plastic map, we carry mortar ammo below our belly into a desperate black.

"Hurry! We're being overrun! Come on, man!"

We can't go any faster. Our engine temperatures are against the red line. Our hearts pound.

"The last round left the tube two minutes ago."

Sweat fans open under my armpits.

We hover overhead. "Where is everyone? Who's left?"

"Just us. We're the only ones!"

"We'll get you out. Climb onto the load!" I yell into my microphone.

"Thank you! Thank you!"

"Eat NATO rice!" French screams, firing like the madman he's allowed to be. His spittle lands on the shell casings at his feet.

We place our sling load next to them. "Get on! Get on!"

As they climb on, they are cut down. I shriek and heave the helicopter in the night sky. I try to crush the enemy under the pallet weight. Nothing matters anymore.

My throat is dry. I'm hoarse.

America.

America.

Life links.

I try to rub the spot off my plastic map with my finger.

Nothing is in color anymore. It's faceless people, dancers, soldiers, gunners, pilots, living in black and white.

An American soldier is bound on his back below me. His mouth is stuffed with rags to keep him quiet. I reach to help him. But I can't.

And I bolt upright.

And sometimes Alesti is bolt upright in his cot across from me. Our bodies are soaking wet and we're sucking air like winded bulls and we aren't embarrassed anymore and we don't look at each other but simply lie back down and go back to sleep.

America.

America.

Sweet dreams, soldier.

The sun once again brings morning through our door. Alesti sits slumped over the edge of his bed, cigarette smoke rising from his face.

"You okay?" I ask.

Alesti nods. "We need better guns."

"We carry .45s. You can't get anything bigger."

"Not bigger," he says, sitting up to look at me. "Better."

"Meaning?"

"Let's go do some trading."

We dress, take a case of C-rations we have stashed behind our wall lockers, and borrow a Jeep for a drive to Tuy Hoa Air Force Base, north of our compound. It's a clear, warm morning, and the forty-minute ride seems short.

We meet with a sergeant who deals in firearms and trade him our case of C-rations for two M2 rifles. The sergeant will trade each C-ration meal separately. It's all the rage to use the top identification flap on each individual meal as a postcard home. Let's collect all twelve, shall we.

On our way back to Phu Hiep, we stop at a shed used as a Vietnamese carpentry shop and take the rifles inside. A man pieces together a child-size coffin, and another works on a bookcase. Neither looks at us. A small, withered man shuffles around the coffin maker and asks if he can help us. Alesti draws the man a picture of an M2 with the barrel cut off and the stock cut off forward of the butt at the hand grip. The man nods, and we hand him the weapons.

We walk outside and light up, sitting on our heels with our backs against the wall in the shade of the carpenters' shack. The temperature rises; the earth warms beyond the building's shadow.

"Great idea cutting those things down," I say. "Was that your dream?"

Alesti ignores my question. "Tape a couple 30-round magazines together, and we've got automatic pistols that shoot .30-caliber for effect. We don't have the hassles of a long barrel or stock," he says.

"I can't wait."

We sit in silence and hear rasping sounds of saws on wood and taps of a hammer or mallet from inside the building.

"I don't want to be here, anymore," Alesti blurts out.

"You mean here? As in Vietnam?"

"Yeah. I've had it."

I don't know what to say. I light a cigarette off the butt dying in my hand. "Maybe you just need some rest."

He huffs. "Sure. Rest. That'll do it. Just a little rest."

"What about the nurse you've been seeing? Can you talk to her."

"I think that's where I caught it. Fran's burned out worse than me. We got naked last night and couldn't even get it done."

Alesti digs his heel through the dirt and buries his cigarette. "Those nurses, all they see all day is blood. Missing limbs. First-hand death. Day in, day out. I don't know how the hell they do it. And us. What about us? How are we supposed to make sense out of it? Hell, I feel like a stranger to myself."

I'm stunned to hear him putting words to my very own dreams.

Alesti shakes his head. "It's being too close to the mistakes. The give backs. The LZ everybody dies for and then we just give the land back. We just move on and do it again on another nameless ridge. Body count warfare; it's making me crazy. And we can't stop it." He lights a cigarette, inhales deeply, and exhales loudly. He puts the cigarette back to his lips, changes his mind and throws it into the trench he made with his boot heel. "We can leave it. We can get back to the States and get our heads straight."

"No, we can't leave. We can't leave until they tell us we can leave." I flip my tasteless cigarette away. "Unless you're holding back and own an airliner or something."

"It's never happened before. Damn, my sex is dying. I don't dream about women anymore. I go to these out of control places. These endless loop nightmares. It's killing me."

"Well, we can't be alone," I say.

"We're rotting, damn it. We're rotting, and we don't even know it."

The old, gray-haired man appears in front of us. He doesn't say anything; he simply looks from us to the coffin in his carpentry shop. Then he squats and hands us our weapons.

"How much?" Alesti asks.

The man looks around cautiously, then writes the number "10" in the sand between us.

I reach in my pocket and take out $10 in military scrip. Alesti does the same. We hand the papasan the money. He takes the scrip, stands and bows. Then he disappears into the carpentry shop. We've probably just funded the local VC brigade.

We stop at a whorehouse a couple blocks from the carpentry shop. Alesti is inside for about twenty minutes.

"You feel better?" I ask.

"I did it twice." His expression doesn't show satisfaction. "I still feel pretty bad."

-16-
Unexpected Reprimand

Riverside, California: Annie

Last week I took my finals. Tonight Bonnie and I will endure bone-chilling wind gusts for her final exam at obedience school. She's come a long way since her first class. A diploma with her score will tell how far.

As we wait for the class to begin, the breeze carries the word "Vietnam" from a nearby trio of women about my age. I adjust my position to listen.

"Oh, no. When?" gasps the owner of a German shepherd mix.

"Monday. We received notice today." The toy poodle owner's expression confirms that the news is not good.

I don't want to hear how bad it is, but I'm mesmerized. My hands shake and I hold my breath. Bonnie seems to sense my tension and leans into my leg.

The Labrador retriever's owner puts an arm around her friend. "How long will he be gone?" she asks.

"Six weeks," the poodle owner laments.

I cough as my exhalation catches in my throat. Gone? Six weeks? Jim's already been gone four months with eight to go. Still, I remind myself, it will be hard for her, too. Although I understand her worry, I can't help but feel a little envy as well.

"Everybody, listen up!" Our trainer's voice ends the conversations.

He calls our attention to a large square of posts and rope that form our show ring in the middle of the basketball court. In turn, we'll go through the exercises. When it's our turn, Bonnie does well enough, with minor glitches while heeling, standing and coming when called.

We line up with our dogs sitting beside us and command them to stay. We leave them behind as we cross to the far side. When we turn to face the line of sitting dogs, I see Bonnie shivering between a large, shaggy dog and a little terrier. Quietly, Bonnie leaves her place in line and trots to me.

For the next exercise, we return to the line. Bonnie and the other dogs lie down on command. Again, we leave them behind. After about one of the three minutes, Bonnie again breaks out of the line and heads for me; a wise move, it turns out, as behind her, the shaggy dog lunges for the terrier.

Bonnie's final score is 115 out of 200, no extra credit given for discretion.

Vietnam

I'm called to Major Guilliam's office.

"Mister Weatherill," Guilliam begins, "most of our experienced warrants have left or are leaving shortly. We need you in Maintenance—Tech Supply to be exact. I'm canceling your aircraft commander orders and moving you there. It will be a better fit."

"Sir?" I swallow hard.

"Your aggressive attitude can be better used there. You're going to Maintenance effective immediately."

"Sir, with all due respect, I prefer to fly. I would rather stay operational," I object.

"I don't care. Flying a helicopter doesn't mean a thing on an efficiency report."

"Major Guilliam, this isn't right."

"You're excused, Mister Weatherill."

I'm confused. I've kept my mouth shut about Guilliam and now I wonder why. If I go to Captain Dodge or

Lieutenant Kase, it will only draw them into my battle. They don't have the horsepower to pass a major. My only recourse is to go to the colonel. I leave Guilliam's office, walk down the hall to our commander's door and knock. I hear a "Come in!" and open the door.

"Ah, Mister Weatherill, what can I do for you?"

"Sir, I don't know where to start. I'm a little scared."

"Start at the top and let's see what we've got."

I start with Guilliam's comments about my flight with Horton and our ground resonance problem. I go to the Silver Star flight with the phony awards I refused to endorse, and Guilliam's threat of a Flight Evaluation Board. Then I recount the meeting I just left and my rescinded aircraft commander orders.

"Why haven't you come to me before?"

"I assumed you knew, Sir."

"Well, I should have. What do you want to do?"

"I'm here to fly. That's what I want to continue doing. I can't win a fight I don't even know how I got into."

"I don't like my officers being treated this way, and especially behind my back. You'll remain one of my aircraft commanders. Thank you for coming to me. I'll take care of it."

I come to attention. "Yes, Sir. Thank you, Sir," I say and leave.

Outside operations I stop and light a cigarette. The enormous weight I felt on my shoulders has lightened. I know I've made a powerful enemy. Still, I feel less encumbered, somehow empowered, cleansed in the confessional.

When I walk into our hooch my posters welcome me like old friends. Alesti is busy writing a letter, so I lie on my cot and stare at the ceiling.

There's a knock on our hooch door.

"Come in," I say.

The hooch door swings open, and CW3 Burrows walks in carrying a paperback book. "Good morning, gentlemen, I hope I'm not disturbing you."

"Good morning, Sir," I return, standing up.

"Mister Weatherill, I was told you're a Humphrey Bogart fan." He looks at the posters of Bob Dylan and Humphrey Bogart on the wall above my bed. "Ah, I see the information is correct."

"Would you like a seat, Mister Burrows?" I ask, and offer the end of my cot.

"No, thank you."

"I'll leave you two alone," Alesti says and disappears out the hooch door.

"Mister Weatherill, I'd like to give this to you." Burrows hands me a paperback copy of C. S. Forester's *The African Queen.*

"Thank you, Sir."

"You know we gave you boys a hard start here, didn't we?"

"Yes, Sir, you did."

"Well, we're from an older school. But I want you to know that what's happening with helicopters in this war will redefine Army aviation. Thank you for coming this far from home."

"I like a challenge."

"Well, life is a tough school," he says and looks back at the posters. "If you don't mind me asking, who's the other man on your wall?"

"Bob Dylan."

"Yep. Never heard of him."

"You're headed stateside now."

"Yes."

I offer my hand, and we shake.

When we leave the hooch, Alesti already has loaded Burrows' stuff in the waiting Jeep.

"Thank you, Mister Alesti," Burrows says and climbs into the vehicle.

PART 6

APRIL 1968

234 DAYS TO GO

17

Mortar Attack

Vietnam

We're in Pleiku for the night. Alesti and I have joined two local pilots in a bar. The entertainment is a couple of Australian strippers we'd chased around the Central Highlands like a posse after Jesse James. Finally we caught up with them, and it's show time.

Alesti's eye lands on a redheaded Australian with a set of wonderfully firm breasts. "Pretty nice, huh?" Alesti winks and licks the air between his face and her chest.

Sellers, one of our local friends, looks toward me and shakes his head. "How can you stand this guy?"

"Practice." I shrug.

Alesti's eyes are fixated on the performance on the stage. He curls his index finger for the woman to come over. The Aussie purses her lips into a pout and holds her breasts in her hands.

"My kind of woman," Alesti declares and sets his glass on the current layer of empties.

O'Neil, the other local pilot, watches with his mouth open, and Sellers takes obvious joy in reaching over and pushing his jaw closed. "You've never seen tits before, O'Neil?"

"Not like those."

Alesti turns in his chair. "Back, boys, take a number."

The place is packed with yelling, screaming, smoking, drinking escapists. Drinking soft drinks behind the bar is the night tactical emergency crew. Being sober probably gives them a clearer view.

Sellers taps me on the shoulder and gestures toward the emergency crew. "It looks like they got a flight."

I turn to see the pilots walking out of the bar. "Bad luck."

"Hell, it was supposed to be quiet. I wonder what's up," Sellers asks.

"No telling. Let's watch the show. We get enough of that and very little of this," I say.

"Yeah, you're right."

For a second I think it's Alesti wolfing air, but the pitch.

"Oh, shit," O'Neil says.

"Incoming!" someone screams. "Incoming! Incoming!"

Sellers twists toward O'Neil. "Let's get out of here."

And then the first rocket explodes into the wall next to the stage. The second crashes behind the stage; the third and fourth outside in the dirt. Now it's an open-air bar, and chairs are flying, and glasses and tables and bodies. Another volley of rockets explodes around us.

Sellers grabs Alesti, and O'Neil grabs me, and we scramble for the door and a nearby bunker. Before we reach the bunker, the attack is over. Now, we go back and help the living. And then, we leave and go back to our tent. And the dead are packed up to go back home.

In the morning, we talk about the night over coffee and grid maps and sortie sheets and enemy movements and eat synthetic eggs and drink synthetic milk and order our fuel loads and extra cans of synthetic turbine oil and look forward to our synthetic potatoes for dinner. You don't look back. You save that for when you get home.

18

It's a Girl

Riverside, California: Annie

This first week of the new semester finds me relieved that I still can fit in the desk. However, the baby isn't due for another two weeks.

"Ms. Weatherill, do you think this poem was based on an actual incident?" the instructor asks.

I want to answer, but a sudden abdominal squeeze steals my concentration and I can't speak.

"Ms. Weatherill?" The instructor looks about the classroom, pauses, and calls on someone else.

My midsection relaxes. Except for the backache I've had for weeks, I feel fine. This can't be labor; contractions are supposed to hurt.

I check the time. We're thirty minutes into the class. I was unable to register for a required class that meets tonight. This afternoon I will ask that professor if he will make room for me. Given my obvious pregnant condition, I doubt he'll want to do anything that might upset me.

Again, something possesses, holds, and releases me. Fifteen minutes have passed since the first one. My back still aches. I decide I should go before things get difficult. I gather my things and leave as gracefully as possible.

Seven minutes later, I'm in the lobby of the humanities building. The professor I need to see is on the second floor. I consider an elevator ride, but choose the stairs and find the office. I figure I could have about five minutes left between contractions to state my case and get out. I knock on the door, and a voice invites me in.

A timeworn face looks up at me above tortoiseshell-framed reading glasses. The man waves his hand toward a chair across from his desk. "What can I do for you, young lady?"

I sit. "I registered for your Milton seminar, but was notified it was full. I can't take it any other time. This is my last semester and I need it to graduate. Do you think you could make room for me, please?" I stand and reach across his desk to hand him my request form, then retreat to the chair. I glance at my watch as he examines the form.

"Well, let's see if we can squeeze you in." He shuffles papers on his desk.

As if on cue, a contraction hugs the baby for a moment, and releases. I breathe slowly and concentrate on keeping a bland expression.

The professor writes on a roster and looks up. "Yes, I think that would be fine. The first class is tonight, you know?"

"Thank you," I smile, relieved to be enrolled and to be able to speak again. I estimate I've got ten minutes to clear a final hurdle. "Do you have an assignment sheet I could take now? I don't think I'll be able to make it to class tonight or maybe Thursday, but I could work on the assignment."

"No, I don't have anything." The professor appears to have second thoughts. He also looks as if he'd probably have a heart attack if I tell him I might be giving birth right now in his office.

"It's an emerging family situation," I explain.

The professor concedes, and I go to my car to wait for the next contraction. Then, I drive home.

Janie is on the phone when I walk in.

"When you're done, I'd like to call your mom," I say.

She looks at me wide-eyed. "Have to go. Talk to you later," she blurts into the receiver and slams it down.

I think I must be quite a sight as I pick up the receiver and dial Marie at her office.

"What's happening?" Marie's voice is cautious.

"I'm fine. I'm having some contractions, but nothing big. I thought I'd let you know."

"How far apart?"

"About ten to fifteen minutes."

"I'll be right there."

I go to my room, pull out fresh clothes, and take a shower. Then, I pack some things, just in case. I include a blanket and a little gown my sister Janice made for her sewing project at school. If it happens today, she'll be thrilled; today is her seventeenth birthday.

Marie and I don't talk much on the way to the March Air Force Base Hospital. I hope she remembered her rosary and her fingers won't be too stiff from clenching the steering wheel as she navigates through afternoon rush hour traffic.

At the hospital, I'm examined and surprised I'm already halfway dilated. I'm prepped and wheeled to a labor room. The patient in a bed across the room stiffens and moans. A man holds her hand.

"Would you mind if her husband stays?" the nurse asks me. "He was in Vietnam for their first baby. This one's six weeks early."

"Of course," I respond, surprised at the question.

Marie sticks her head around the door frame, and we invite her in. She asks how I am, and I say I'm fine, except for a backache.

A nurse takes my left hand to insert an IV needle and misses her target. She tries a little closer to my wrist and misses again. "You have rolling veins," she grumbles. She moves around the bed with her IV stand, and takes my other hand.

"That's your problem," I manage to gasp through a contraction. She reminds me of a mosquito whining for a place to land.

Marie rubs my back and finds just the right places.

My entire being now focuses on delivering a baby. I barely register the wails from the other bed. I'm calm, sailing in the center of my universe with my baby. We ride the turbulence and float during the slack. If they leave us alone, we'll be fine, I tell myself.

"This will help you relax," says a nurse with a hypodermic needle in one hand. She reaches for the IV tube with the other.

"I don't need that. I am relaxed. Don't ...," I protest, but it's too late. The hypodermic's contents soar into my veins.

Marie steps out to grab a bite with Fred. Janie drops in to wish me luck before she heads home. Tomorrow is school for her. They seem to think it will be a long night.

"How much time between contractions?" a voice breaks into my bubble.

I really have no idea. I squint at the wall clock. Without my glasses, I can barely see the hands. Worse yet, it's military time; my civilian mind can't tell the hours from the minutes. When a contraction starts, I look at the clock. By the time the next squeeze comes, I've forgotten when the last one ended. I watch the fastest blur make a circle. The next hand to move should be the minute hand. Yes, I think I see it, maybe. "Ten minutes," I venture a guess.

"It doesn't matter," whispers the beguiling drug that now plays games with my mind.

I agree. When they ask, it will be ten minutes for now. I retreat into my universe to flow in harmony with my body.

Some contractions later, a woman examines me. My dilation is progressing.

"How much time?" the voice asks a couple of contractions later.

"Five minutes," I guess for a while. The contractions seem closer, and then I guess three.

I don't know how much time passes. Cries from the other bed cease as the woman is wheeled to the delivery room. I endure repetitive interruptions and physical exams until a doctor breaks my water and bursts my peaceful universe.

A tsunami of pain capsizes my emotional boat.

"Aaaahhhooow!" I hear a primal wail. It's a new voice. I look around and realize it's mine.

I'm helpless against the maelstrom that compresses my baby and pushes its head against the birth canal. My worse pain is thinking my baby may also hurt and I can't do anything about it. My lungs howl in protest. The rest of me is along for the ride as time slides by.

"Let's go," says a voice at the foot of my bed.

In the delivery room, I transfer from the bed to the delivery table. I'm given a spinal injection before I lie on the table and put my feet in the stirrups. Within seconds, I'm numb below the waist.

"Push," orders the doctor.

I do my best, but I can't tell how hard I'm pushing or even if I'm pushing at all. It's as if the lower part of my torso isn't there.

"Push! Push harder," he urges.

Over and over I try.

I hear a rusty hinge creak as if someone opened a door. I look for the sound and realize, over my deflated belly, that my baby's face has hit the air. The doctor syringes out the mouth, and the rusty hinge produces the most beautiful sound ever.

The body and legs follow the head into the world. I get a glimpse as a nurse whisks the little hollering bundle to a table on the other side of the room. I don't see the curly dark hair I expected. I'm eager to hold my baby.

"What do I have?" I ask.

"A girl," says the doctor.

I laugh. Jim was right. We have a daughter, Maryanne Marie. It was Jim's idea—Mary for my mother, Anne for me, and Marie for his mother. I watch with longing as she's wheeled out of the room.

Buried Alive

Vietnam

> *Brandishing lighting swords,*
> *A Samurai thunderstorm quake*
> *Roars into the timbers.*
>
> *Pests run by hunched over,*
> *Birds fall from the sky,*
> *Trees rip from the ground by air.*
>
> *As the storm abates*
> *The roar becomes quickly muffled, distant.*
> *The fresh adrenaline air becomes heavy.*
>
> *My thoughts return to silence.*
> *Settling dust allows light*
> *Back into the bunker.*

*   *   *

It's 11 p.m. and moonless. We land bone-tired at Holloway after three unrelenting days of resupply. Our heartbeats tell us we are alive, but our souls don't seem to exist. Like a cancer, they are black from death. We stumble to the scummy showers and back to our tent. Lights are taboo; we navigate by our glowing cigarettes.

Inside our tent, we pass sleeping pilots from some imported slick company. We're glad our bunks are the last two at the other end of the commune. We can drink and whisper and drink some more, then maybe sleep.

I don't care that my boots are wet. My feet are covered with foot rot, and one more day won't change things. I slide my feet out of my boots and pull on my pants. I dry my feet. I can put them back in my sweat-soaked socks, go barefoot on the red dirt floor of the tent, or put them back in my wet boots. I pick my boots. I've packed around a bottle of Johnny Walker Red while waiting to be a daddy. Annie is due soon. I'm ready to celebrate. Beside me on my pillow is my custom M2 cut down to a pistol, and I reach over and pet it, almost expecting it to purr.

"I'd like to climb in tub of scotch, and have a woman caress me," Travis says as he puts his towel over his shoulder and pulls on his pants.

It sounds like someone whistled at his comment. The whistle tone changes. I drop my cigarettes and lighter in a boot, grab my gun with one hand and the scotch with the other.

Travis hears, too.

"Incoming!" we yell.

Two men sleeping at the other end of the tent snap up. Rockets transform the night into a dirt and metal rainstorm. We help five slick pilots escape out the end of the collapsing tent and dash to a bunker. Above us in the night sky a four-star, red cluster bursts—the worst possible signal. We are overrun.

I push Travis down the stairs, on the heels of the slick pilots. A grenade explodes as I dive into the darkness and land on Travis, who has landed on someone else. The grenade blows half the stairs down on us. The bunker is pitch black and filled with the pungent smell of spent cordite. I feel blind, lost.

"Come on!" Travis grabs my arm.

We go deeper into the ground. Outside, a crack and bang like lightning and thunder sends a pressure wave across us. The top of the bunker falls in, and we're buried. I can't breathe. Travis' hand lets go. I arch my back to find space. I push harder, and my back stops against one of the planks that supported layers of sandbags and pierced-steel planking.

I feel frantically for Travis' legs and come up with his boots. My hands follow along his body. Travis is curled in the fetal position. His head has to be right here. He coughs. A weak "shit" comes out of the black.

I find his arms and follow to his fingers. In his right hand is his .45.

"Hell of a place to bring me for a drink, Weatherill."

Questions flash through my mind: *What now? Where is the air? What's happened to the other pilots? Why are my legs burning?*

I feel a wall against my back. "Push with your feet. I'll move the dirt away," I say.

We work a long time to open a corner of the bunker.

"I sure wish we had a light," Travis says.

"I had my smokes tucked in my boot when we strolled in here." I sift through the dirt along the fractured beams and find my M2 and the scotch. After a few minutes, my fingers touch the metal of my Zippo, and then my pack of cigarettes. I sit back against the wall of the bunker and light up. I pass the cigarette to Travis, then open the Johnny Walker Red and savor the liquid taste.

"You suppose we ought to dig a hole to the outside? Air really isn't free," Travis says, looking around with his cigarette.

I hand him the scotch and move to the highest point in our small lean-to. I find a splintered chunk of wood and dig at the sandbags while Travis pushes the dirt away with his feet. After some effort, we have air.

"There really must be a God someplace," Travis offers. "To wherever He's hiding." He toasts and takes a gulp of scotch.

"With any luck He's made a hole near us," I offer.

I try to wedge my head between the sandbags and the

collapsed roof of the bunker to look outside through our air hole, but I don't fit. The earth shakes from a huge explosion and dust falls into our small space.

"Either the ammo dump or the fuel dump," Travis guesses.

I push the stick into the air hole and light another cigarette. "Who do you suppose is going to win this thing tonight?"

"Them." Travis takes a pull of the scotch and trades me for the cigarette. The tip of the cigarette glows from the draw of his lungs. "Am I bleeding, too?" he wonders aloud.

"Draw on it again." In the light I see the spots. "It must have been the grenade."

"Probably."

I tear a strip from the towel Travis carried in here, and pour some scotch on it. In the glow of the cigarette I dab and pick small slivers of steel out of him.

"That stings like hell."

I tip my cigarette to his face and draw in. "You'll have a chance to get even."

We hear pops of rifle reports. Boots pound across the top of our collapsed bunker. Dirt sifts down in a fine mist and settles on the small damp spots on Travis' legs. "Fuckers," he mutters. "I want to kill 'em."

They're just doing their jobs, I think, and I'm instantly disgusted with myself. *I'm an idiot. They're trying to kill me. They're trying to kill Americans tonight.* "A lot of that going on," I whisper. I find a large shard and pull it.

Travis moans.

Someone jumps on the bunker. I snuff out the cigarette.

"Sorry," Travis whispers, catching his breath from the pain.

The man on the bunker is silent for a moment and then we hear his footsteps as he runs off the collapsed roof. Seconds later, an explosion shakes the bunker and the air becomes dirt again. I cover my face and listen hard. It sounds like a telephone. My mind is blank. I feel myself choking and lose track of time. The ringing comes again but there's still no picture in my head.

"Breathe, damn it! Breathe!" Travis' voice urges.

I take in a short breath. It tastes gritty.

"They must have heard me and tried to finish us off. Man, I'm sorry," Travis whispers.

"Don't be. They probably smelled our cigarette smoke pouring out the air hole."

"Damn, I never thought of that."

"I hope the guys on the other side of this collapse are okay." I turn toward our air hole. "Is it over?"

"I don't know," Travis pauses. "I was out, too."

I suck a deep breath through the hole in the night, then push away and sit back against the bunker wall. "I don't like this place." I light a cigarette and cough red dirt and smoke. Then I inhale deeply on the cigarette again, lighting up our cave.

"Well, right now it beats being up there." Travis presses his face against our air hole, shifts his position, and listens. "I think the Spooky ships are out. Six thousand rounds a minute ought to kick some ass."

"Plug it up!" I make the cigarette glow and look for the scotch.

Travis shoves the chunk of wood in the hole and sits against the wall.

I think I'm scared. My mind is blank. I can't even remember what my wife looks like. Or my father. Or my mother. In the cigarette's glimmer I find the scotch and open it.

"My grandfather says fear is black, and you push it out by thinking of snow," Travis says. "I could go for a blizzard right now." He laughs. "It would definitely help cool things down."

"My grandfather was an immigrant from Sicily," I say. "My mother is first generation off the boat." That little piece of information seems a long way off—the near past so far away it might as well be on the moon. My ears ring like mad.

"And look where we are, in the middle of somebody's civil war," he says.

"Are we even on the right side?" I feel pressure on my chest, and throw my cigarette away.

"They're trying to kill us; it's a moot point." He finishes the cigarette and snubs it out on a sandbag. "We're doing what our country asked us to do." He takes the scotch and drinks and becomes silent. Travis is asleep.

I find the bottle before it spills.

We went in the bunker just after midnight. We're dug out eight hours later. We walk through the remains of our tent and see bullet holes in our cots where our sleeping bodies should have been. I pick up a spent bullet for good luck.

Outside, Travis takes pieces of shrapnel out of me while we contemplate drinking a bottle of George Dickel we found in our commune tent. The owner won't mind. We'll make it up to him later, surely. We see the Huey pilots are out, too, searching through the ruined tent.

We find a medic who sews up our larger cuts, and then we head for the remains of the briefing room. On the way, we run into Bridger, our gunship pilot friend we haven't seen for almost six weeks.

"If you want to get even," he says, "we need a couple copilots."

Travis and I exchange looks and thank Bridger for the invitation.

"Good to see you, men," the C.O. greets us as we enter the briefing room. "We've got one Chinook flyable. I'm taking it to Phu Hiep for parts. We'll have a second one ready in three to four hours. The two of you will fly it."

"Sir, the gunship platoon needs some pilots. I'd like to crew for them," I say.

"Sure, so would I, Sir," Travis adds.

"You're the only two here to fly the second ship.

Everybody else is headed for Chu Lai to get some of the Boxcar machines. Don't get lost."

"Yes, Sir. In a couple hours then, Sir."

Travis stares at me. "You really want to do this?"

I grab him by the arm and we head to Bridger's hooch. "New recruits reporting."

Few words are spoken. We follow directions and within forty minutes of entering Bridger's hooch we're airborne, a flight of three Huey gunships. Our objective is to find the people who shelled and mortared us.

We fly up a narrow river canyon that breaks open into a large grass clearing shaded by a handful of trees. We're not expected. A couple hundred NVA sit, eating their rice in the morning sun.

"Hey, Hog, you got them?" Bridger radios.

"We're on them," the pilot answers. The Hog is a Huey that carries twenty-four rockets on each side. The rockets are a mix of goodies, some white phosphorus, some anti-personnel, some high explosive, all designed to kill.

The Hog rolls in with morning death. Bridger and I cover the left side of the Hog's flight path. Boyd and Travis fly on the Hog's right. Our Hueys carry fewer rockets, but each is mounted with a Gatling gun. Bridger and Boyd fly the Hueys and fire the rockets. Travis and I fire the Gatling guns. The door gunners hang out the side doors of the Hueys, firing machine guns.

Halfway through the Hog's run, the NVA bolt for a waterfall a couple hundred yards farther north, at the end of the valley.

"Break off, Hog. Break off!" Bridger orders.

"Yeah, the waterfall," the Hog pilot says.

Travis and I open up with the Gatling guns, catching the NVA soldiers in their race for the waterfall. Dozens of bodies go down. God, the power.

"Let's go. Break off!" Bridger orders.

The Gatling guns go silent.

All three ships turn around and regroup downstream of the waterfall. In a deadly V formation we fly up the canyon. About a hundred yards from the waterfall, we expend every last rocket and bullet we carry into the pristine setting.

We pull up hard and flee for the cover of the jungle above the falls. There's a small explosion below us and then a larger one and then one so large the entire waterfall collapses.

The eternal process of erosion, the story of all dirt eventually flowing to the sea, is helped by some young men from America riding in helicopters. Who said we never did anything constructive?

Our excavation complete, we return to Holloway. Then we're sent back to Phu Hiep on the coast. About twenty minutes from base, the C.O. comes on the radio.

"Seven Zero, Windy Six, over," he calls.

"Seven Zero, go ahead."

"Get on the scrambler."

We flip the proper switch. "Seven Zero is up, Sir."

"We've got some good news for you," the C.O. says.

"We leave tomorrow. Packing isn't allowed." I brave a wild guess.

"No."

"So?" I say.

"What do you want?"

"A ticket to San Francisco."

"Think about it. What do you want? Does boy or girl give you a hint?" the C.O. asks.

"Wow! Really?"

"Well?"

"I don't care," I answer.

"Come on. Every father wants a son."

"Okay, a son."

"Bingo! Your wife is doing fine, too."

I'm on cloud nine, maybe ten. I roll the helicopter all over the sky, climbing, diving, and pedal turning. Travis shoots from his cockpit window and the door gunners fire in celebration with my cavorting. We soar over the airfield with three colors of smoke grenades duct-taped to pieces of parachute cord dragging behind us in the sky.

On the ground, we talk party. I put $50 on the bar. Fifty dollars will buy about ten gallons of whiskey. People aren't going to run out of spirits. I sit at the bar and read the message from the Red Cross, scribbled on the back of a page from the company radio log. I'm the proud father of a six-pound, eleven-ounce baby boy.

The next morning, I limp my hangover to the ten-by-ten shack we call the PX and buy the only box of cigars that say "It's a Boy" on the wrapper. Everybody gets one. I smoke one myself. Evening comes. We're at the bar again.

The war slides into a slack period, like a referee somewhere blew a whistle. For the next few days, we carry ammo, food, clothes, beer, soda, toilet paper, and all the other sundries firebases need to exist. We hit Nha Trang on the way back to Phu Hiep and pick up a load of mail.

It takes the company post office a couple hours to sort the mail, enough time to get out of war clothes and into something resembling what we look like in America. Into the center of the hooches comes the mailman.

My mail consists of a tape recording from home and a square, flat package from my brother. I feed the spool onto the tape recorder and push the play button.

"Hi, Son, I want to tell you that my new granddaughter is absolutely beautiful." It's my father's voice.

"Huh?" I stop the tape and rewind it. I push play again.

"Hi, Son, I want to tell you that my new granddaughter is absolutely beautiful."

I stop the tape again. My head drops into my hands, only one thing on my mind: a letter I sent to Annie after the Red Cross telegram. In it, I rave about the ball glove and baseball bat I'm going to buy our son; the fishing poles and footballs and motorcycles; and I feel like shit.

First, I write another letter to Annie telling her I'm even happier about having a daughter. Then, I go to the

C.O. and raise holy hell about the Red Cross. They had a fifty-fifty chance.

I go back to the PX and buy the last box of "It's a Girl" cigars and pass them out. I go back to the bar and buy for the house. Somewhere, after the second or third scotch, it gets all scrambled up. Everybody thinks Annie and I have twins.

Hoarse from trying to explain, I head for my hooch. I fall on my cot for a nap and realize I haven't opened the package from my brother. I've written and told him about the destruction of the Falcon kite and the Captain America still sitting behind the concertina wire in the mine field. I expect to find another kite in the package. Instead, I find a stack of blank typewriter paper and a book on origami: how to fold different paper airplanes and birds, things that will actually fly.

I flip through the pages looking for something large enough to carry me across the Pacific Ocean.

Riverside, California: Annie

I'm a walking blues song. Thanks to post-pregnancy hormones, I'm euphoric and terrified and despondent— sometimes all at once—and my milk came in and soaked my blouse during class.

Jim just has to know about Maryanne by now, I try to convince myself. The Red Cross lady came to my hospital bed and promised to send a message that day—the same promise my mother heard when I was born. My father has yet to receive that telegram.

The suspense is agonizing. Finally the mailman brings a letter from Jim. I rip open the envelope. The letter is dated four days after Maryanne's birth.

> *Dearest Annie and Son. An eloquent gift! A son! Oh, Annie, I'm so happy. I was floating all last night.*

Well, the Red Cross was half right.

20

Points of No Return and a Baptism

Vietnam

In everyone's life or a nation's history, there are points of no return. For a pilot, it's when you pass a line on your chart that makes it impossible to return to your starting place. You simply don't have enough fuel. For a nation it's when you try to kill an idea, especially when a nation has an overabundance of hate.

I'm sitting in my hooch. Someone knocks on the door.

"Come in."

It's Sergeant Steele, our crew chief. "I'm sorry to bother you, Mister Weatherill, but I need to talk to you."

"Please, come in. How can I help you?"

"I got a letter from my mom. It's made me afraid." Steele pauses and takes a letter out of his fatigue pocket.

"What's happened?"

"Martin Luther King has been assassinated."

"Yes, I heard. Please sit down." I offer up Alesti's cot. "What does your mother say?"

"Riots all across America," Steele says, sitting. "Let me read you something in her letter. 'Son, I'm sad that you are in this war. Dr. King encouraged disobedience to the draft. I know you love your country, but does your country love you back? Be careful.'" Steele puts the letter back in his fatigue pocket and shrugs.

"My mom's a thinker," he says, lighting a cigarette. "If she's afraid, it's normally for a good reason. She sees more and more men like me getting out in our society. We're changing things. Things are getting better, but she's afraid of retaliation." He draws on his cigarette and then exhales.

"My uncle says I should stay with what I'm doing. He's proud that soldiers like me are making strides. He and my mom are brother and sister. He says she can be a little gloomy every now and then." Steele takes a deep breath. Tears overflow from his eyes. "Why did this happen, Mister Weatherill?"

"I'd be a liar if I told you I understand. America is killing the voices that speak to its humanity, and somebody is making it happen. The future is the only place we can find them, but, first, we have to make it there."

"What are we supposed to do?" Steele wipes his eyes.

"I didn't let my country down and you didn't either. If you and I can shake hands and go on, maybe it'll spread. Maybe the rip in America can be mended one handshake at a time."

"Thank you, sir." Steele stands. "I appreciate you talking to me. You're a real gentlemen. You can always count on me."

"I know I can." I reach out and we shake hands; the first stitch in the torn fabric.

Every year leaves fall off trees. I wonder what it felt like to be the first person to see it happen. Did they believe it was the end of the world? Probably; why wouldn't they? History is the only seer, and it only looks backwards.

Riverside, California: Annie

As a non-Catholic, I was required to take instruction with a priest before Jim and I could be married in his church. I welcomed this opportunity to learn about Jim's faith, but I began to suspect it involved something more. During one session, the priest explained that procreation was the purpose of marriage.

"Do you know of any reason you would not be able to have children?" he asked.

"I don't know if I'm able to have children or not. I've never tried to get pregnant." I was surprised by the question.

His expression indicated that he expected to hear something else.

I also was required to sign a statement that I would not interfere with Jim's practice of his faith.

Now, it's Easter. The same priest who performed our marriage sixteen months ago is baptizing our procreation. Maryanne is oblivious to the promises, prayers and blessings made on her behalf. She looks like a porcelain doll in the gown my sister Caty made. Janie, holding our sleeping baby, beams, having been promoted from Jim's little sister to Maryanne's aunt and godmother. Fred stands in as godfather in place of Jim's brother. Marie and I stand aside. I feel Jim's absence and try to imagine him standing beside me.

After the ceremony, the priest observes aloud to nobody in particular, "I see the marriage appears to be working."

"It's hard to argue when we're on opposite sides of the world," I respond.

Fred stifles a grin and puts his arm around my shoulder.

21

Long Night in the Central Highlands

Vietnam

We are sent northwest from Pleiku to Dak To as the sun disappears behind the western mountains and darkness seeps into the valleys. We refuel and hear it will be the last fuel at Dak To. While the fuel hoses are pulled, twenty American troops with a lot of ammo climb on board. A dusty, unshaven lieutenant, hands me a map and stands fascinated by the cockpit glowing back at him. The red light bathing our instrument panel washes his face. He pushes a finger into the map.

"So you want to go to Dog Bone?" I say.

He nods. "Okay if my men smoke?"

"Yeah."

Firebase Dog Bone sits on a small ridge that resembles a bone when seen from the air. The cannon positions are on the high ends of the ridge, and the heliport is in the middle saddle. It's two kilometers southeast of firebase T-Bone. These firebases provide mutual fire support.

"They're in trouble. It isn't going to be nice," the lieutenant warns.

"We suspected that." My stomach constricts. We're a long way past my Worry Line. I pull a pack of cigarettes from the pocket on the front of my body armor and offer him a smoke. "Well, get comfy. We'll be about thirty minutes."

"These things will kill us," he says, lighting the cigarette.

"Yes, but it takes years. Bullets are noticeably quicker."

"Sure," is all he says before he walks to the back of the Chinook and takes a seat.

The helicopter is heavy. We pull in maximum power and just sit there. After almost a minute, we rise to a hover. I breathe forward on the cyclic stick and we ease ahead, inches off the ground. Our front wheels bang the dirt a couple times during the acceleration through translational lift, and then we leave the planet.

Dog Bone has a complement, on bright sunny days, of about 200 men. When we leave Dak To, the firebase already has suffered significant casualties. Chatter on the air-net frequency for our mission and calls for help tell us it will be a long night for American soldiers.

We push our helicopter to the limit, first due west for twelve kilometers, then south down a mountain valley. We fly just under the clouds, concealed in the darkness and rain. All our lights are off except our instrument lights so low we barely see our gauges.

We are a flight of three Chinooks. I'm in the first machine with Mister Frost, who has less than thirty days in country. He's on loan from a Chinook company in the south, somewhere around Saigon. We need a dozen more pilots and only get one. Behind us is Alesti with Kase. Peters is in trail with Travis. Floating with us on our mission are two gun teams in C model Hueys. For about twenty minutes we feel half safe.

"Frost, listen," I say to my new copilot.

"Listen?"

"Steele, you got it?" I ask our crew chief.

The radar on the enemy's large guns causes a beep on the FM radio. When we hear the third beep we know a round is on the way.

"Yes, Mister Weatherill. Everybody, brace yourselves!" Steele yells to the passengers.

Bewilderment glares back from many grunt eyes.

I bank the helicopter hard right and push the nose into a dive. "We're being tracked. Check FM," I call on the air-net frequency.

"We've got it," Alesti answers.

"Us, too," Travis' voice cuts in.

The air around us fills with explosions of radar guided rounds. The explosions are blinding white, then spent, cordite gray smoke; we all know the sky around the light is full of shrapnel. The gunships roll away to attack flashes coming from enemy positions. We fly on.

At T-Bone, Hueys have dropped brilliant white parachute flares that turn night into day on the firebase. The light will identify enemy movement and help helicopter pilots see where to land to deliver supplies and passengers. As we pass over, a Huey departing the T-Bone heliport is hit and flames erupt from the engine compartment. The aircraft noses down, gaining airspeed, and flies a tight circle back to the firebase. It lands at the edge of the heliport, and the crew jumps out. The men scramble for safety as the Huey slides backwards off the heliport into the tree line and tears itself to pieces. The mission goes on.

Dog Bone is dead ahead, lit up with parachute flares and exploding rockets like a Chinese New Year celebration. Cannon muzzle flashes thrust fiery tongues into the night. Dozens of rifle barrels send tracer lines into the jungle. We start our approach. Ahead, on the Dog Bone heliport, a shoulder-fired rocket hits a Jeep mounted with a 106 mm recoilless rifle. We are waved off. We fly over the Jeep; its operators are motionless in the burning vehicle.

"We've got to get that Jeep off the pad!" When the firebase radio operator keys his microphone the roar of gunfire fills the earphones of our helmets.

We apply maximum power and claw for altitude to climb out of the light of the attack. We bank left and head for the relative cover of a nearby rain band illuminated by white parachute flares above Dog Bone. The engine temperatures can use the cooling rain.

"Push that damn Jeep over the side!" someone yells over the air-net frequency.

Our gunners shoot into the night at the tracer fire aimed at us. Suddenly, the Chinook shudders. The right engine is hit. The fire light comes on as the engine erupts in flames, exposing us in the murky sky. The right fuel tank ruptures. Fuel sprays out and ignites as it reaches the burning engine. The shrill from the fire bell floods the cockpit. We look like a comet.

"The outboard side of the engine is burning!" Jacaby yells, hanging out the right gunner's port. "Fuel's pouring aft from the tank." A line of tracers comes out of the trees across the right side of our rotor system. "Assholes!" Jacaby yells and returns fire.

Yellow and red cockpit warning lights flash on.

"Hey, Seven Zero, you're on fire, man!" It's Alesti.

"The grunt lieutenant back here wants to know what to do, Sir." Steele sounds scared.

"Tell him to bust out the windows and join the fun. How's the left side, French?"

French fires back down the tracer lines. "Heliport's clear, Mister Weatherill!" he yells.

"Take short bursts, French, or you'll melt that thing!" Steele calls out.

"Okay! Okay! I'm sorry; I wasn't thinking!"

"Don't think later, you fucker!" Jacaby scolds.

The grunts break out some aircraft windows and open fire into the jungle night.

Alesti comes on. "The heliport's clear. We'll cover. Keep it turning! Keep it turning!"

"Frost, you've got the aircraft. Keep the turn going." I'm about to pull the fire handle out to shut the fuel and oil valves to our burning engine, when I realize we won't make Dog Bone on one engine.

"How we doing, Steele?" As I speak, ground fire hits the helicopter's belly.

"The engine's burning good, but I can hear it running. We're losing lots of fuel, and, Sir, some grunts are hit pretty bad; two near the engine are dead."

I look at Frost. His face is pale, his eyes fixed straight ahead. I look at our instruments. We're not turning; we're descending into oblivion.

"Why?" Frost mutters.

Alesti's voice bellows in my ear. "Turn, you son-of-a-bitch. Turn!"

I grab the controls and bank hard left. I switch the landing light on for an instant. We're inches above the jungle, aimed at the side of a nameless ridge. The controls feel frozen. "Jacaby, get up here!" I call.

"Who are they?" Frost yells.

The steep bank clears the trees and we continue our fall back toward the lower valley.

"Come on, Jacaby, Frost's freaking!" He has a death grip on our flight controls. I need help. Tracers lick out of the trees at us, and I turn off the landing light.

Jacaby shouts at a grunt. The grunt thrusts a grenade launcher in Jacaby's chest and takes Jacaby's place at his machine gun, yelling profanity in time with the bursts of the weapon.

Jacaby appears in the companionway to the cockpit and looks at Frost. "Goddamn punk."

"He's glued to the controls," I say.

Frost screams something incomprehensible.

Jacaby raises the butt of the grenade launcher and drives the wood stock into the side of Frost's helmet. "Let go of the goddamn controls, ... Sir!" Jacaby looks at me and grins. "When we make Dog Bone, let's leave this dickweed on the ground."

I wish it were that simple.

Frost turns his face to me. "We're going to die," he declares and passes out.

"Not tonight, shithead," I mutter.

The Chinook holds together through our violent turn. We line up on short final and impact on the heliport.

The smoldering wreckage of the upside-down Jeep on the slope below our chin bubble is grotesque. The two dead soldiers, their clothing ablaze in gasoline, lie beside the dislodged recoilless rifle

"Everybody out! Let's go!" Steele yells.

The three wounded are unconscious. The two dead are slumped on the floor. Fifteen men scramble down the ramp and try not to look at their dead comrades.

A medic comes out of nowhere and loads five wounded on our burning ship.

"Hey, no free rides. This thing's not going to fly far," Steele says. "Wait for the next bird. This one's just going someplace to die."

"Die here, die there, what's the difference?" the medic says.

"Seven Zero, you getting out of there? We're right on your ass. Twenty seconds. C'mon! C'mon!" Alesti calls.

"Boss, the medic convinced me. We're taking five." Steele reports.

"Get out of the way, Seven Zero," Alesti calls again.

"Get on, Steele, fast. We're leaving!"

Ed Frost appears to revive, but it's a false start. He moans and collapses against the right side of his chair. Death is supposed to be a lot easier if you're asleep.

The engines come to full power and the Chinook leaves the ground.

"Hang on!" I call as I pitch the nose down.

We dive off Dog Bone, and the blades carry us into the darkness. As we pass out of the white light from the parachute flares, the right engine explodes.

Steele rushes to the cockpit. "Can I help, Sir?

"Pull the number two fire handle. Shoot both bottles. Let's get that fire out," I say. We aren't setting any records, but the trees are still below us. Thank God for mountain valleys.

No one cares what time it is, only that there's time to continue breathing. We stagger south for Kontum. Number one engine runs like a dream. If I could meet the people who put that inanimate collection of metal together, I would kiss them all.

Kontum, at our reduced speed against headwinds in the pitch black of night, and without running into anything, is thirty-five minutes away. We know it's still there, on Earth, the oasis, the mid-ground between Heaven and Hell. When we get there, we'll get cozy in a bunker and help defend Kontum. Hell of a plan.

"Windy Seven Zero. Windy Seven Zero, Windy Nine!" Alesti calls on the radio.

"Seven Zero," I respond.

"We thought we lost you! We saw an explosion."

"Number two blew up," I say.

"Where are you?"

"Southbound, trying not to run into anything."

"Everybody okay?"

"No."

"Mister Weatherill," French says, "a little right, Sir. This ridge is getting pretty close."

"Thanks, French."

"Look, Nine, we're a little busy, gotta go."

"God speed, partner," Alesti says.

The light from French's cigarette lighter flashes behind the companionway. "Ya know," he says, keeping the mike keyed as he draws on his cigarette, "My roommate left today. He's gone back to the world."

Steele, standing in the companionway, lights two smokes and puts one in my mouth. Then, he hands me the worn cotton rag hanging out of his back pocket. I wipe my face.

French walks into the companionway behind Steele, pulling his intercom cord along. He keys and you hear him inhale through his cigarette again. "He did his time."

"Look, asshole," Jacaby starts, "the bastard was so trigger happy everybody had to carry extra ammo."

"You know, Jacaby, you're fucked," French says.

"I'm under a hundred days to stateside and you're telling me. What you smoking man?" Jacoby retorts.

Steele turns in the companionway toward French and Jacaby. "You keep this bird honest or you stay behind," he says.

French walks to his gun port and tosses his cigarette out into the night. "I'm not toking. Besides, I'm out of here this month."

"Out of here when?" I ask.

"Soon."

"Jesus!"

"I didn't want people to know, Sir. Didn't want to jinx myself," French says.

Jacaby reaches for his groin and gives it a tug.

"It's over, Jacaby," Steele says. "I'm going aft to help the medic, Sir."

"Okay, Steele."

And we proceed south. Kontum Approach answers our second call. "Windy Seven Zero, be advised we're fogged in and still under attack."

"The radar still up?" I ask.

"Affirmative, I can give you a radar assist. Be advised the runway is unusable. It's been heavily mortared, and we have reports of wreckage along the full length. Landing will be at your own risk."

"We've got to try," I say.

"Squawk 6,000, and ident."

"Six thousand, roger." I repeat and enter the numbers into our transponder. Now Kontum is able to track us on the radar screen.

"Radar contact, fifteen west. Fly heading one one zero, downwind leg," Kontum Approach directs.

"Heading one one zero, roger," I say.

"I'm going to take you to the east. It'll be a quick base to final turn. If you need to go around, it'll be straight ahead. Climb to 5,000. You confirm?"

"Five thousand. Instructions understood." We proceed, the voice from the radar room easing the nervousness out of our stomachs word by word. We're given lower altitudes when we turn base, then final approach.

Then, the voice aligns us with the runway. "One-half mile from touchdown, maintain present altitude, on course. One-quarter mile, on centerline. One-eighth mile, runway should be in sight."

It's there in the murk.

"We've got the runway," I declare.

The wheels hit the ground. We're doing 75 knots.

"Twelve o'clock! Twelve o'clock!" French and Jacaby yell.

The wreckage of a Huey and a Jeep emerge out of the fog. I pull the thrust lever up, spooling the number one engine to full power and push the nose over moderately fast. We are airborne again. A twisted tail-rotor blade on the Huey digs along the belly of our Chinook as we labor to fly. Then, the fog opens for fifty yards. The runway below teems with VC. Jacaby and French open fire.

Steele fires the M-79 grenade launcher out the left gun port as fast as he can load. In seconds we are back in the dense fog, fleeing.

"Kontum Approach, Windy Seven Zero," I call. There's no answer.

"Kontum Approach. Kontum Approach, Windy Seven Zero, come in, over." We're talking to ourselves.

"How we doing on fuel, Sir?" Steele asks.

"Cold beer in Pleiku in thirty minutes," I answer.

"If it's still there," Jacaby adds.

"How's the medic doing with the wounded?" I ask. There's no way to change the mood.

"We're up to five dead, five hanging on," Steele says.

I reach under my body armor to pull my last Italian cigar out of my sweat-soaked fatigue jacket. I light up and inhale deeply. A wave of pressure pushes through my eyes. I move my right hand down to the radio console, turn the UHF radio knob to the preset emergency frequency, and key the microphone. "Windy Seven Zero is transmitting on guard. Any station please respond."

"Windy Seven Zero, this is Atlas. Go ahead, Sir." Atlas is the call sign of Pleiku Approach.

"Atlas, Windy Seven Zero is a Chinook en route from Kontum. We are declaring an emergency," I respond.

"Windy Seven Zero, Atlas advises you to land at Kontum. Weather here is ceiling 200 foot overcast with rain, visibility one-quarter mile, over."

"Unable, Atlas," I say. "There's no response from Kontum Approach."

"You squawking 6,000?" Atlas asks.

"Affirmative."

"Radar contact, thirty-nine kilometers north. Say altitude." They've found us on their radar.

"Thirty-eight hundred," I respond.

"Climb and maintain 9,000. Say nature of your emergency."

"Climb is impossible, Atlas. We're down to one engine; we may have fuel for thirty minutes. We have five wounded on board." I leave out the dead.

"Can you make 6,000 feet?"

"I don't know. We'll try."

"Fly heading 180. It is imperative you do not lose altitude."

"Understood. Heading 180; we're on it now."

"Windy Seven Zero, be advised, you are number eleven for priority handling."

"It sounds just like a barber shop number," Steele comments.

"You want to argue with him?" I ask.

"No, Sir"

"It's been a long day, gentlemen." I take a deep breath. I want a cigarette, but I'm out of smokes.

"You falling apart on us, Steele?" Jacaby asks.

"I'm horny, and I'm hungry, and I'm thirsty, and in half an hour we won't even have enough JP-4 to burn my ass." Steele stomps off to the back of the ship. "I need a vacation," he mutters.

"Quiet down. Let's defuse back there." I feel the same as Steele. I want to cross back to the safe side of my Worry Line.

Pleiku Approach moves us around in the sky and has us on the ground in thirty minutes. When we touch down, we run out of fuel. We have enough inertia to roll off the runway, keeping it free for other sweating, desperate souls.

"Pleiku tower, Windy Seven Zero is clear of the runway. Medical assistance, please," I say into the radio.

"What taxiway are you on?"

"We're in the grass between taxiway three and four. This aircraft is out of commission," I tell them.

"Medical help is on the way."

Ambulances take our wounded and our dead. We climb out of the helicopter and walk around to look at the charred remains of the number two engine. I lag behind. Unnoticed by the others, I kneel, grab a handful of grass and kiss the wet, green blades. I get up, look at the clouds above us, and nod at the sky. I throw the grass blades in the air. The helicopter held together through the fusillade. It's hard to believe we left Pleiku only four hours ago. Maybe we've landed in a different century.

A Huey hovers out of nowhere and picks us up. Ten minutes later, we're parked in the Huey's revetment at Camp Holloway. Ed Frost is up and about now. He can't remember anything but a ridge and trees coming up fast. He says he thought he was going to die when everything went black.

Steele walks up to the people listening to Frost. "I think something flew into the cockpit. It must have knocked you out."

"I'll buy if anyone's thirsty." Frost offers.

Thirsty as we are, we all decline.

PART 7

MAY 1968

204 DAYS TO GO

-22-

Game of Cards

Vietnam

Travis and I level off at 3,000 feet above the coast and turn south. We look forward to spending some time on our own base in Phu Hiep.

"Traffic at eight o'clock," Wellish, our new left door gunner, calls out. He's replaced French, who took the Big Bird and his foot rot to America. Wellish has been working in the motor pool and heard stories from the door gunners in his barracks. He says he wants to see the war first-hand from the gun port of a Chinook.

"Who is it?" Travis asks.

Jacaby peers around Wellish. "One of ours," Jacaby says. "Looks like they're coming over for a look-see."

I turn up the volume on the company frequency and Alesti's voice shows up. "How does lobster sound?"

"Delicious. Done for the day?" Travis asks.

"Yep. Cards and whiskey and lobster. Any takers?"

"What about us?" Jacaby cuts in.

Johns, Alesti's crew chief, pulls down his pants and moons us across 100 yards of Vietnamese air. "We don't forget our friends," he transmits on the radio.

"I ought to put an M-79 round up your ass!" Jacaby yells back.

"You keep teasing me, Jacaby, and I'll be coming to your hooch to collect."

"Promises, promises." Jacaby laughs.

The rest of the ride home is relaxing with company alongside and the coast below us. We land in Phu Hiep and park in our revetments. Then we head to the operations room for debriefing.

At the hooch, Alesti has the whiskey poured. It tastes sweet and hot.

"Here's one for you," I toast my poster of Humphrey Bogart and go back for another drink.

The Chinooks in our company work resupply missions all over central Vietnam, from Dak Pek in the north to Phan Thiet in the south. We often don't see one another for weeks. We hear about each other, and maybe catch a word or two on the radio. We can just as easily meet as we can misconnect. For me the pleasure in not crossing tracks with Morrow is superb. I hear he's still bitter about our encounter in the showers.

I haven't seen Alesti since he was screaming for me to turn toward firebase Dog Bone. He hasn't had it easy. Roger Allen, Alesti's roommate in flight school, was killed, along with his crew, while they flew their gunship in protection of an insertion. The loss of a gunship's protection equates to losses on the ground. Alesti throws down two more shots, pushing Allen's death deep down inside.

I look at my friend and wonder what's next for all of us.

We adjourn to our officers' club. It's time to play cards.

Mel Isaac, one of our pilots and our company artist, waits at the card table. He normally draws a caricature of each officer for Big Bird eve, the going away party we hope to have on our last night with the company. The pictures hang on the bar walls. Isaac had a brother in country. "If two Isaacs can't end this thing, it can't be done," was their slogan, until we got word his brother died in a crash east of Dak Pek. Isaac gave up slogans, but fortunately, not his art.

Sitting next to Isaac is Morrow.

Travis looks at the attendees at the table. "Surprise, surprise."

We sit and set up our little nests for the poker game. Alesti looks at me and I shrug.

Lieutenant Kase shuffles, cuts, burns a card, and deals the first hand. As the game progresses, and the night progresses, and the drinking progresses, the stakes progress, too. We're at no limit blackjack.

I have the deal. Morrow puts out $200 and comes up with eleven. He goes down for double. When he puts the second $200 on the table he pulls his .45 automatic from his shoulder holster and puts the pistol on the table, too.

"Pretty melodramatic, Morrow." Travis nods at the pistol and smirks.

"Shut up." Morrow turns from Travis back to me. "Deal, Weatherill."

Alesti sits ahead of Morrow and asks for a hit. He gets a ten of diamonds, considers the addition for a moment, then asks for another hit.

The deck serves a jack of spades. Alesti looks around the table. "Too much I guess," he says but doesn't throw his cards in.

Morrow bolts to his feet. His chair flies back from his knees and hits the wall as if he'd thrown it. "You cocksuckers are setting me up!" he screams and reaches for his .45. His hand catches the pistol grip like a vice. "Well, I'm not going to let you steal my money."

Every eye in our little club is focused on the table.

"You need to settle down, Morrow," Isaac observes softly.

"Stay out of this, Isaac." He lifts the pistol from the table.

I can't stop myself. "You out, Morrow?"

"Yeah, Weatherill, I'm out." He looks around the bar, again making sure everyone knows he's out of the game.

Alesti, his face a Madonna smile, drinks a swallow from his glass of whiskey. "Before you start blowing people away you might want to see something."

Morrow looks from me to Alesti, and then at Alesti's cards. Alesti rolls his hand. His down cards are two aces.

Morrow stands for what seems like forever, staring at the aces. Finally, he looks up. "Fuck you." He looks around. "Fuck you all." He reaches out, grabs his $400 off the table, and backs toward the door like a man robbing a bank.

"Hey, Morrow," I call. I slide the top card off the deck, reach my hand out to the middle of the table, and turn the card face up. It's the king of hearts. If Morrow had stayed in, he would have won big.

"You know what your problem is, Morrow? Huh? You don't have any guts." I reach back and slide the next card off the deck. I throw it to the center of the table. It's the queen of clubs.

Morrow backs against the club door and grabs the knob with his $400 hand. I throw the deck of cards at him, and the cards burst against the air like bats fleeing a cave. Morrow slides out the door and screams into the night. The door hangs open, and we watch him holster his pistol. He spits in the sand.

"You know, I've been thinking of trying to make peace with that guy," I say, honestly. "Looking over both shoulders is really exhausting in a war zone."

Alesti looks across the table with the Madonna smile still on his face and tosses me a new deck. "Deal, I'm still behind."

Kase gets up and closes the door. "I don't know who's crazier, Weatherill, you or Morrow."

Riverside, California: Annie

It's hard to balance being a wife, mother, daughter-in-law and student all at the same time. I try to write something to Jim every day, but finding time and energy is like scrounging for change in the bottom of my purse. I might find a dime or only a penny.

Carrying four classes last quarter was rough. I worked hard but always felt I was behind. I was shocked to learn I somehow made the dean's list.

This term I have three classes and a newborn baby. Maryanne is perfect. I couldn't ask for more. She's calm, happy and fell right into a four-hour meal schedule. However, it takes at least an hour to feed, burp, and change her. This gives me three-hour intervals, providing she doesn't have gas pains in between feedings, to do everything else. When the only sleep I get in twenty-four hours is a series of naps, it's difficult to even think straight, not to mention write a coherent, newsy letter.

Furthermore, living with parents has its advantages, but privacy is the price. It's hard to communicate only through letters and tape recordings. Sharing Jim's letters and tapes with his family limits what we are free to say to each other, and stifles discussion of mutual decisions that should be private.

When Jim left, everyone agreed to an honor system that personal messages for my eyes and ears only would appear at the end, but I'm uneasy. I hesitate to bring up or ask him about something personal because it's likely his response will not remain between just the two of us. This tiptoe approach creates a distance as unsettling as the miles between us.

Vietnam

I'm walking behind a mamasan, who whimpers and holds her right ear. Her hair is matted with blood. I speed up to help her. The woman looks behind, sees me coming at her and bolts. When she releases her ear, I see half is gone. While I run, I reach into my pocket to get my handkerchief to use as a compress, and the woman flees around a corner. When I round the corner, she's gone. It's impossible. Beyond the corner is open ground with no place to hide, but the mamasan is gone.

Someone laughs. I turn and find Morrow standing in his hooch doorway with his razor in his hand. Behind him I hear a whimper. Curled on the floor at the foot of his bed is the mamasan. Morrow walks over and kicks her. She curls tighter.

My body shakes. My hands clench into fists, and I lock my jaw shut.

Morrow walks back to the doorway, holding a razor in his right hand.

I explode at him with my fists as hard as I can swing.

He slashes me with his razor.

My stomach burns. I strike again.

He slashes quickly two more times.

"Bastard!" I scream. My stomach is on fire. "Bastard!" I fly at him again with my fists. There is pain and blood.

I'm shaken roughly. Shaken again.

I open my already open eyes. There is no blood on my poster of Bob Dylan. No blood on Humphrey Bogart.

"Wake up!" Alesti screams. "God, where are you, Weatherill?"

I look around.

Alesti shakes me again.

Now Travis is here. "What's going on?"

I come out of my nightmare. Alesti lets me go.

I look at my stomach. It's covered with sweat. I put my head in my hands.

Alesti lights two cigarettes. "Bad dream, huh?"

"Yeah, you could say that." I take a cigarette and draw a deep breath. Morrow takes up too much space in my mind. A drop of sweat falls from the end of my nose onto the tobacco tube and drowns my smoke.

23

A Ticket Home

Vietnam

We pilots live buckled to a machine that flies—a huge flying truck—and we recognize our friends in the air and on the ground. We learn how to pick a voice out of ten conversations and know who it is, how he feels, and almost the last time he's had a bath.

Randy Brock is one of these voices. He's a rigger for the 173rd Airborne at the logistic pad north of our base at Phu Hiep. The log pad is in the center of a wide, level stretch of sand. We hover in and get hooked to loads too heavy to fly. As we strain to get in the air, Brock climbs into the sling load. With sand and rotor wash blowing around him at almost a hundred miles an hour, he throws boxes off until the load leaves the ground. Then, he jumps free, and off we go. He does it for every helicopter having trouble getting airborne. His exploits for a maximum launch are legendary.

While launching a Chinook with a piggyback load of ammo and a 105 mm cannon, Randy falls, collides with the cannon barrel, and breaks a bunch of ribs. Laid up from his acrobatics, he takes over the log pad radio. It's like tuning into a 50,000-watt rock station. He's clear, concise, and totally organized. He talks us into hovering one more minute at full power and guarantees the load will lift. Then, he charges a six-pack of beer for his efforts as a third pilot. Everyone pays.

Logistics pads move with the war. Just after Tet, we have trouble getting productive loads off the old infantry pad in downtown Pleiku. Some pilots, after getting chewed out for not working well with others, avoid the pad as though it were a Petri dish of plague cultures.

We want Brock to clean things up. Our colonel sees to it, and two days later Brock's smooth Southern voice is on the radio.

Things change, and after a week of work, the pad is back on schedule. Then, Brock is beaten severely by jealous unknowns. The pilots who know Brock start dragging their feet going to and from the logistics pad. Everybody complains to the C.O. again, and a sweeping change of personnel occurs. The pad goes back to work, and supplies get transported.

There's a spooky period when the Grumman Mohawks with side-looking infra-red sensors pick up large numbers of NVA coming down the Ho Chi Minh Trail. To defend our positions, some wizard in headquarters decides to put a firebase west of a village called Polei Kleng, due west of Kontum. The firebase will go on a high point close to the Cambodian border and rain artillery shells day and night—a new American weather system.

Our mission is to move the firebase away from Kontum and put it in the mountains at the edge of eternity. We hook up to our first gun and ammo and stagger off under the weight. Halfway, we call ahead to the base.

"Mile High, Windy Seven Zero. Anybody home?"

"You mean the only help we get are a couple broken down Windys?"

"Brock, I thought you were kissing nurses in Pleiku."

"I filed for divorce. I'm out of the log pad business. I do firebases now. What you got?"

"Number one cannon with ammo."

"Well this is going to be complicated. We want the number one gun in the number one hole. Think y'all can handle that?"

"We hear you're still a virgin, Brock."

"I'm waiting for a certain general's daughter."

The move continues all day. In the afternoon, thunderstorms come in and add a little flavor to the grind. For the last sortie on our sheet, Alesti and I takeoff side-by-side from Kontum. His external load is a conex, a big metal box full of radios and electronics to coordinate firebase Mile High's effectiveness. We carry two Jeeps inside our cavernous body. Each Jeep is mounted with a 106 mm recoilless rifle.

We line up on parallel approaches, Alesti going for the center of the cannons to place the conex in a hole dug for its protection. I approach the heliport fifty yards to Alesti's left. We land and lower our ramp as Alesti comes to a hover above the conex hole. Brock is having a field day with Alesti.

"I saw a donut dolly fly a Loach better than this. Y'all sick, Windy?"

"You guys are all the same. You keep trying over and over to put a square peg in a round hole," Alesti pushes back.

Four men on the corners of the conex lead it down into the hole.

"Hold on, Windy; the hole's jammed by a sandbag," Brock says. "I'll pull it clear."

"What'll it cost?"

"A ticket home. Hold on."

Lieutenant Kase and I watch Brock jump to the side of the conex and pull the sandbag out of the way. His four helpers hold the conex still.

The first of our Jeeps is out. The two grunts manning it rev its engine and drive up the short road to the first cannon position. As soon as the Jeep stops it's hit by a rocket, blowing Jeep and men in all directions.

"Incoming!" I yell into the radio.

Alesti has the conex half in the hole. Bullets, explosions, pieces of people and dirt fill the air over the firebase.

"Don't be gentle, Windy, let her settle!" Brock urges. "Release! Release! Get the hell out of here!"

Dozens of men in black clothes swarm out of the timber at the edge of the clear zone around the firebase. The second Jeep is out, and Jacaby calls our right side hot, shooting to protect Alesti's ship.

The attackers open fire, and Alesti's machine takes rounds in the belly. His gunners fire straight down.

"We can't release! Hang up! We've got a hook hang up." Alesti's voice shoots over the airways.

"Down two! I can reach it! It's twisted tight on the hook jaw!" Brock yells into his radio.

Alesti lowers. His crew chief and Brock are eye to eye at the cargo hook hole.

Brock grabs the eye of the sling and twists with all his might. Alesti's crew chief pushes the sling-eye free.

A man in black pajamas steps out from the timber and aims a shoulder-fired rocket at Alesti's Chinook.

Brock is nineteen when our radio friendship starts. He's nineteen when he throws himself off the conex into the rocket. He's nineteen when he explodes and pieces of his body land beside the man who has killed him. Nineteen, not even old enough to vote, when he gets his ticket home.

Jacaby fires dozens of rounds into the man in black.

We fly from Mile High to Camp Holloway, refuel, and fly on to Phu Hiep. I feel like a witness to murder, fleeing in disbelief, looking for an amnesia cloud.

When we return to Phu Hiep, Alesti goes over to the Evac hospital and picks up Fran, the nurse he's seeing. They come to our hooch, and we sit together. She talks out her death events and listens as we talk about Randy Brock. We're too numb to cry.

Afterwards, Travis and I go to the bar. I know Fran and Alesti make love because Alesti smiles a few times the next day, just out of the blue. Good for them.

24

War Gets Personal

Riverside, California: Annie

Mother's Day dawns early, bright and hot. Maryanne's thoughtful and most appreciated gift to me is almost an entire night's uninterrupted sleep. When I change her diapers, she smiles and tries to laugh. Later, I find a box of candy in her crib.

Jim's mother, Marie, enjoys her presents and a long-distance phone call with her mother. The conversation starts with a loud Brooklyn accent and breaks into Italian. Then I call my mother to wish her a happy holiday.

Mid-afternoon, the phone rings.

"Annie, it's Jimmy!" Janie screams. "He's on the phone!"

I race to the phone. Janie hands me the receiver as Marie skids to a stop beside me. I hear a low static sound.

"Hello," I breathe into the receiver.

"Mrs. Weatherill?" a man's voice asks.

Janie jumps up and down, and giggles, as Marie yells a list of questions into my free ear. Fred pops on and off the extension.

"Yes," I say. I can barely hear or understand the man.

"Mrs. Weatherill, I have a connection to James Weatherill. When you are through speaking, say 'over' and wait for him to speak. Over."

"Okay, over," I respond.

"Hi, Annie. Hi, Ma. Happy Mother's Day. Hi, Janie, Dad. Over," comes the familiar voice across the lines and airwaves.

I want to tell him how much I love him and how proud I am of him and to congratulate him on being put up for instructor pilot, but I just can't concentrate with all the commotion.

"I love you. How did you do this, over?" I swallow the lump in my throat.

He says something about standing in line for five and a half hours. The confusion and voices around me drown most of his words.

I attempt a few more comments back and forth, and frustrated, I hand the receiver to Marie. "Say 'over' when you finish talking and wait for him to speak," I tell her. Then, I sit on the couch to wait for another chance.

Marie talks and Fred chimes in on the extension. Eventually, Marie calls me over and hands me the phone to say goodbye. The line is dead. I place the receiver on the cradle and squeeze my eyes shut.

Regardless of the frustration, it's a treasured moment to know Jim is fine at the exact time we hear his voice. We all agree it's the best Mother's Day present ever.

Vietnam

Captain Dodge, our platoon leader, has an unending love of the female form. For his hooch decorating project, he sends hundreds and hundreds of dollars away in white envelopes for magazines that come back in brown ones. He posts a sign on his door that reads, "I'll kill anyone who enters before the grand opening." We all give Dodge's hooch a wide berth.

After a few weeks of sharing our hooch for card games, music, and stiff drinks, we hit at him for an explanation of his mysterious behavior.

"Just wait," is all we get.

Fortunately, when Dodge announces the grand viewing, most of us are home. We set up a bar on a picnic table outside his hooch. Rather than just push the door open for all to enter, he takes us in one by one.

Finally, he takes my arm. "Come with me, son."

I follow him into his hooch and don't remember swallowing for at least ten minutes.

He wallpapered everything in his hooch with nudes cut from the porn he'd ordered; his walls, his sink cupboard, his chair, his bed posts, his lamp shade, his everything. It's the most incredible sight my eyes have ever seen.

I walk out to the picnic table and pour a glass of scotch. The bottom of the glass is the next thing I realize I see.

We all clap in congratulations. Everyone wants to move in with Captain Dodge.

Riverside, California: Annie

It's more than a hundred degrees outside this morning and getting warmer. I wish we were in Lakewood at my parents' house. Today is my mother's birthday, and it's cooler near the coast.

Maryanne's cheeks are flushed, and she looks sad. Portable electric fans provide meager relief. Maryanne gulps down a bottle of water. She wears only a diaper, and I wipe her head and body with a damp cloth. I hope nothing will make her cry, because crying will only make it worse.

In the afternoon, I dip Maryanne in the kitchen sink to cool her off. She kicks and pushes with her feet and tries to stand up. She's slippery, and I have to keep hold of her and support her head, too. I put her dripping naked body on a towel on the counter and let her kick. She stares and coos at her reflection in the toaster. Then, I put a diaper on her and move her to the couch.

Maryanne is on her tummy next to me while I work on a school assignment. She kicks and squirms, and suddenly rolls from front to back for the first time. I grab her and run to the phone to call my mother to wish her a happy birthday and give her this exciting baby news.

Tomorrow morning, Maryanne and I will venture out to buy my ticket to Hawaii. It's a hard decision to leave her behind for the week. She's growing so fast. Every day brings something new. I want her daddy to see his baby and hold her and get to know her while he has a chance.

Jim and I, also, are changing and growing. He writes:

> *It sounds like maybe I'm searching for something but, or should I say well, I am. I am trying to keep the me you knew before I left.*

New responsibilities during this dissembled relationship have taken their toll, and there's more to come. We want to grow up without growing apart. We agree we need the time to focus on us; to see each other and hold each other and be more than letters and disembodied voices on tape recordings.

During our week in Hawaii, Maryanne will stay with my parents and sister Janice. I hope we've made the right decision to leave our daughter behind.

Vietnam

Two Chinooks leave for the Phu Cat Mountains to carry Koreans on an assault. One of their firebases has taken fire from a nearby village, and it's time to get even.

Dodge and Miller land next to Travis and me in a cemetery outside the Vietnamese village. We hover next to one another, with our rear wheels on top of large stone slabs that cover family vaults.

Soldiers are fighting hand-to-hand about fifty meters ahead of us. Our gunship cover can't keep the VC heads down without also shooting Koreans. We've stumbled into something big.

"Jesus!" Travis points between his legs.

Two vault slabs beside our ship's nose slide sideways.

"Under us! Under us!" Wellish yells. "VC under the nose."

Our load of Koreans is slow exiting our helicopter.

"Steele, what's the hold up?" I call.

"Sir, they're fighting right behind our ship. It's like we landed on an anthill. They're everywhere."

Wellish and Jacaby open fire as men gush out of the ground.

I reach over and take my M2 from its holster at the side of my seat. Two VC climb out of a tomb beside the cockpit and look, first at the Chinook, then at me. As they swing their rifle barrels toward me, I push my cut-down M2 out my window. The end of my trigger finger attached directly to the adrenaline pump in my heart, I see their faces and I fire.

My Worry Line has disappeared behind the cockpit.

"Everyone's out! We're empty!" Steele yells.

Travis pulls on the thrust lever and the blades take us straight up. He pedal turns to the east, and we flee for Qui Nhon and the coast. No one aboard is hit. No one is wounded. We cheer to release the choking tension. Dodge and Miller are out behind us.

We reload with fuel, ammo, and Koreans. Daylight is dying and the news of hand-to-hand fighting on the battlefield arrived in Qui Nhon ahead of us.

A new Korean interpreter comes to the cockpit with a map of the village. "Sir, we are fighting hard here and here." He points to the locations. "These troops need to be here." He looks up at us. The new "here" is in the middle of everything. Our interpreter doesn't realize we have just come from his "here."

"Do these guys think we're a tank?" Travis asks.

"You take here?" the interpreter points again.

"I'm getting that impression." I look at the Korean. "Yes, we go there."

"Sir," Steele calls.

"Go ahead," Travis answers.

"Mister Travis, these guys look like they just got off the boat."

We finish loading. A Korean lieutenant comes to the companionway, and speaks to our interpreter. They agree on something, and the lieutenant walks away.

"We go now, okay?" the interpreter asks.

"Steele, Jacaby, Wellish, everybody ready?" Travis asks.

"Ready, Sir," they answer.

As we fly to the battlefield, we scrutinize the Koreans' map. We will land on a road between the cemetery and the village. We listen to the air-net for the sortie, and hear only calls for men, ammo, and Dustoff.

It's night now. At the Initial Point, the IP, the point in the sky where we begin our approach to a battlefield, we call on the air-net that we are inbound.

"Windy Four Seven, Air-net Boss, hand-to-hand contact in the cemetery and the village," Boss informs.

"Thank you for the update, Boss. Two minutes out," I answer.

"Ready?" I call aft.

"Ready left. Ready right. Ready ramp," they respond.

As we touch down on the road, a rifle report blasts from the cargo area.

"One of these assholes just fired a round through the ceiling, Sir," Jacaby says.

"We've got a leak! Spray coming from the centerline overhead," Steele calls. "He got one of our hydraulic lines!"

Our cockpit hydraulic gauge tells us the rest; number one system quantity and pressure fall to zero. We're down to one flight hydraulic system, in the middle of a hand-to-hand battlefield, loaded with soldiers so scared they don't know if their rifle safeties are on or off.

The ramp is down, and the soldiers stream off our helicopter. The door gunners don't fire in fear of hitting a Korean. We hear a rap on the side of the cockpit. The

Korean lieutenant has brought the culprit soldier to the
nose of the ship. He pistol whips the man and leaves him
on the road.

"We're clear! We're clear!" Steele calls.

We go to maximum power, and depart on a direct
heading to Qui Nhon. Our ship is broken. We're done for
the night.

Steele has our Chinook repaired by morning, and for
the next two days we resupply the Korean forces clearing
the village and the surrounding area. We also bring
blivets of fuel for the Korean tanks and armored
personnel carriers blasting the village back to the Stone
Age. The cemetery is transformed into a rock quarry; the
dead VC soldiers transformed on a funeral pyre.

Phu Hiep looks good as we break over the runway and
move into trail formation for recovery at the heliport. We
park in our revetments and gather to congratulate each
other for being alive. We count our bullet holes for any
new records and set the meeting time for the party at
Captain Dodge's hooch.

A maintenance sergeant walks up to our cluster.
"Four new pilots got in yesterday."

"Maybe I can get a day off." Travis smiles.

"Dreamer." Alesti smirks.

From hand-to-hand combat to maybe getting a day off
without bleeding for it, all within three days, must be a
new company record.

Dodge throws his flight helmet in the air. "Party
time."

Off we go to debrief and then to our hooches. Our
smiles feel awkward. We disappear inside our respective
holes and shed our battle clothes.

Suddenly, an unearthly yowl cuts through the
hooches. We all bolt for the central open area. Dodge is
rolling in the sand, strangling one of the new pilots.
Peters and Kase are the first on Dodge, prying the new
guy free from his death grip.

"What in the hell's the matter?" Peters shouts.

Dodge looks up from straddling the newcomer on the ground. "This motherfucker's scraping off my wallpaper."

"It's filthy and offensive," the new guy answers between fits of coughing.

Dodge fires his right fist like a bullet into the new guy's nose and blood pours out.

Everybody jumps Dodge and pulls him off. "You're going mental on us, leader," Kase yells.

"He had no right. Son-of-a-bitch! Who do you think you are?" Dodge shouts at the bloody nose.

"The Bible is full of sinners like you," the new guy preaches, holding a cloth to his nose.

"I'm going to beat the hell out of you, you self-righteous prick," Dodge counters.

Peters, Travis, Styki, Miller, Kase, Alesti and I drag Dodge bodily away from the fight and into our small officers' club. We force gin into him until he calms down. We guard him and keep him drinking until he's had enough to pass out. Then, we carry him to Peters' hooch and put him to bed.

At precisely 11 p.m., four unknown avengers sneak into Dodge's hooch, throw a blanket over the new guy, and tuck him in tight. On the way out of the hooch, the avengers set off a smoke grenade. After about thirty seconds, the new guy runs, coughing, from the hooch. The next morning, he requests a transfer out of our company. The C.O. considers it and signs the order.

*   *   *

The sun is out and the sky is clear blue. A black ant walks across a checkered blanket spread on the wild grass. A man lies on the blanket. He wears body armor over his T-shirt. An open wicker picnic basket holds a homemade peach pie inside. More black ants climb onto the blanket from a grass bridge. Red ants scout the opposite edge.

The man sits up, startled by an unaccustomed noise. He sees the ant armies; red ants at one side of the blanket, black ants at another. The sound the man hears is their marching feet. He reaches for his gun.

And I know this is another dream. And I have tried to drink myself into the oblivion of sleep. I don't want to dream anymore, but it has started, anyway. I sit up in my bed, and ants are everywhere. I open my eyes, but the dream doesn't end. I grab my gun and start shooting. But nothing happens. No bullets come out. And I look at my posters. But my walls are blank, and I itch, and ants are in my hair and in my ears and in my nose and in my mouth, and I cough and I spit and I slap furiously at my body.

Then I'm awake. I hope I'm awake.

I'm lying on the grass in the shade of our helicopter. Two ants are tugging at the crumbs on the bottom of my C-ration cookie tin. I give them a few drops of leftover syrup from my can of C-ration peaches and wish them well.

Riverside, California: Annie

It's almost midnight and I've completed my assigned reading. All I have to do is write another fifteen-page paper in a week. It took three weeks to do the last one. Then, I have a final, and school is out.

In spite of my efforts, there will be no graduation ceremony for me. This quarter I was forced to admit I was overwhelmed and something had to give. I dropped a class and broke a promise. Now, I'm just one class short of meeting graduation requirements. Sometimes small numbers can be so big.

Breaking a promise to myself is hard, but worse is breaking a promise to my father. When I decided to drop out of college halfway through my senior year to marry Jim, my father took me aside.

"Why," he asked, "can't you finish the year and get married the following June as you had planned?"

I explained that I would go back and finish my degree while Jim was in Vietnam. We wanted to be together as much as we could before his deployment. If we waited until June to be married, we would be apart while I was in college and he was in flight school. Instead of almost a year together we would have only a few months before he left. Then we would have an additional year of separation.

"I'm worried," my father began. "When you change paths, priorities change. It can be hard to go back." He paused. "Many people don't."

"I have a timeline. When Jim goes to Vietnam, I'll go back to school. I'll be twenty-two years old when I graduate. Most people graduate at twenty-two without taking time off. I will do it. I promise."

I did go back and almost made it, too. I know "close enough" isn't "good enough" for my perfectionist father but I think he'll make an exception when I tell him I've arranged to take a correspondence course for the remaining credits. I don't need a cap-and-gown ceremony.

After I take my final exam, I'll pack up Maryanne and Bonnie and drive to my parents' home. My mother and sisters can hardly wait to get their hands on Maryanne. My father doesn't say anything, but I've seen the sparkle in his eye when he comes to Riverside to see her.

I'll leave Maryanne and Bonnie in Lakewood when I go to meet Jim in Hawaii in July. I'm worn out from being torn in so many directions. I look forward to becoming whole again, even for just a week.

PART 8
JUNE 1968
173 DAYS TO GO

.

25

Promotion and Change of Command

Vietnam

I'm past the halfway point of my tour. I try not to think about 173 days; bullets don't care what day it is.

The commanding officer calls me to his office. When I walk in, I see Major Guilliam and Captain Dodge. I come to attention at the colonel's desk. I'm puzzled. I've been too busy to get in trouble. For the last three weeks all I've done is fly and study for the instructor pilot exams. Yesterday, I took the oral and finished the flight test with the group standards instructor. We seemed to get along.

"At ease, Mister Weatherill," the C.O. says. He looks at Dodge. "Captain."

Dodge clears his throat. "Mister Weatherill, we want to congratulate you for your accomplishment. Effective immediately you are endorsed as an instructor pilot on the Chinook."

The C.O. comes around his desk.

"Major Guilliam has already assigned check rides for you to perform," Dodge continues. "The general is coming through Phu Hiep, and you will give his pilot a currency ride. Then they'll continue south. Again, congratulations."

"Thank you, Sir," I say. "What time?"

The C.O. puts his hand on my shoulder. "Major, Captain, gentlemen, you're excused. Mister Weatherill a word with you." He walks back to his desk and sits. "The general is supposed to be here at 2 p.m. His pilot is all yours after that. Use the general's Chinook." He leans forward and puts his hands on his desk. "Mister Weatherill, I would like to give you some advice." He stops and cocks his head at me. "Stay optimistic. I like that about you. Don't let rank or years of service push you around or dilute your standards." He sits back in his chair. "And for God's sake, son, remember lives are at stake. If a pilot needs to be pissed on, then make him wet."

I'm flattered by his confidence. I reach over the desk, and offer my hand. "Sir, yes Sir."

We shake, and he signs an order on his desk.

"I believe you have work to do, Mister Weatherill."

"Thank you, Sir," I say coming to attention. I walk into the sunlight and stand. I'm fourteen again and dreaming of flying. I love what I do. *Focus*, I tell myself; *I can do this.*

The staccato beat from the blades of a Chinook landing at our heliport rousts me. I get my flight equipment and head for the aircraft. I salute a lieutenant colonel who walks up to me as I arrive and drop my flight gear on the aft ramp of the Chinook.

"I guess we're flying together," he says.

"Yes, Sir, I'm Mister Weatherill."

He shakes my hand. "Let's get this over with, shall we?"

After the oral discussion of the Chinook's limitations, we preflight the helicopter, start up and takeoff. In the traffic pattern, the lieutenant colonel attempts to fly the aircraft without the stability system engaged. He's unable to control the Chinook and I reinstate the system. After a few minutes, I fail an engine. He's slow to react and seems unfamiliar with the emergency checklist. I reinstate the engine and we land and taxi to the revetment.

I look across the cockpit at the man I'm giving my first official check ride. "Sir, this did not go well. How about we eat dinner and fly again in about two hours?"

"I've been flying all day, Mister Weatherill. If you will excuse me, I am done with this day."

"Colonel, Sir, you've had the general's life in your hands all day."

"And your point is, Mister?"

"Sir, you're not going any farther in this aircraft unless you're sitting in the back as a passenger. Your performance was substandard."

"We'll see," he says and leaves the aircraft.

I fill out the paperwork for the check ride and walk to the operations room.

The general stands outside. "Well, how'd my man do, Mister Weatherill?" he asks.

"He failed, Sir."

"Oh? And why is that?"

"As long as the flight was uneventful, he was fine. Toss in an emergency and he was so far behind, he might as well have been in Da Nang," I say.

"This is a lieutenant colonel we're talking about."

"Yes, Sir."

"Now, what, Mister?" the general asks.

"Sir, Major Guilliam can assign you a pilot."

"I need to go now. You can take me," he says.

"Sir, I don't have the authority to just leave," I protest.

"I do, Mister Weatherill." The General turns and walks into operations.

"Yes, Sir," I mutter to his back.

Something is not right. We're airborne, southbound for Cam Rhan Bay. The general acts as copilot. The lieutenant colonel sits in the back, smoking a cigar. *How can a general's pilot bust a check ride?*

We land at the logistics pad and shut down the Chinook. I get my gear and step off the helicopter. I see the general and the lieutenant colonel standing alongside the aircraft.

"Mister Weatherill," the lieutenant colonel says, "I want to shake your hand. You rarely see a WO1 rated as an in-country instructor pilot in the Chinook. In fact, you're the only one I know of."

As we talk, a U-21 airplane is towed onto the ramp behind our parking spot.

I know I've been had, but I don't know why, or how. "What gives, Sir?" I ask.

"I had my doubts," the lieutenant colonel continues. "The general didn't. Congratulations to you, Mister Weatherill." He offers his hand.

"Mine, too, the general adds. Get in the U-21; it'll take you back to Phu Hiep."

"Colonel, Sir?"

"Yes, Mister Weatherill."

"You're still busted."

*   *   *

Our commanding officer catches the Big Bird home, and Isaac's handiwork immortalizes his face on the wall of our small bar. Rather than the usual caricature, Isaac paints a formal portrait, a proud picture of a compassionate man.

The colonel leaves a void behind. He was like an uncle with the power of life and death. We'd get in trouble and he'd get us out. He knew things before we'd even brought him the message, plus he got Guilliam off my back. Now, he's gone.

There's a knock on our door. It's Captain Dodge.

Alesti and Travis walk in behind him with two six-packs. "Hello, Sir," Travis says.

"Mister Travis, Mister Alesti."

"Is this official or friendly?" I ask.

"A little of both," Dodge says. "Before the C.O. left, we talked about Major Guilliam. I thought I'd bring you men up to speed."

"The C.O. was a good man, but we could never figure why he didn't do anything to Major Guilliam after he weaseled out of the Tac E," Travis says.

"I wondered the same thing," Dodge replies. "The colonel told me Guilliam thought he got away with it."

"It seems like it to me," Travis interrupts.

"Hold on a minute, now, Mister Travis. The colonel said he had to wait for the right favors to come due. As you know, the regular officers in this Army have a branch specialty. In my case, it's artillery. Flying is my current assignment, but I can go back to artillery any time I request it."

"This sounds too good." Alesti licks his lips.

"Guilliam's branch is infantry. As of tomorrow morning, he's the new commanding officer of the infantry company that's going in to relieve the guys at LZ Tara."

"God, the snake bit himself in the ass." Travis grins and looks around.

I nod my head in awe of our old commander. "The cagey old fart."

"Tell me we got the insertion," Alesti says.

"They're going up by convoy on the coast highway," Dodge answers.

"Even better." Travis nods.

"Let's all keep away from Guilliam tomorrow morning, okay?" Dodge waits for his words to sink in. "Okay?"

I nod my head in agreement.

Alesti bends his beer can in half. "Time to celebrate."

"Sir, one question," I say. Everybody looks at me. "Sir, what about the citations Mister Peters put in? The citations I've put in for my crews?"

"All of us have written citations," Alesti adds.

"They're history. They've disappeared. There are no citations," Dodge says.

"But, Lieutenant Drum?" Alesti asks.

"Lieutenant Drum denies any culpability. He says he sends everything on. My guess is that somebody downgrades the citations. But we can't prove anything. Gentlemen, I've got a sortie to take out. I'll see you in a few days. Keep your heads down."

The three of us stand as Dodge leaves.

"Parts ended right, but there's a lot wrong here," Travis says.

"Sit down." Alesti rubs his chin. "We'll be there in the morning."

"Dodge said to let it go," I say. "We won."

"We have to see this through. No loose ends." Alesti lights a smoke.

"Kase and Styki need to be here," I say.

"They're supposed to be in tonight. I'll wait up," Travis offers.

At 6 a.m., with the sun rising over the South China Sea and a light breeze bringing in the morning, Major Guilliam walks out the door to his hooch. On the boardwalk in front of his door Travis, Alesti, Kase, Styki and I stand with folded arms and say nothing as we watch Guilliam move his belongings to the Jeep he has parked nearby. He climbs in and drives away.

Riverside, California: Annie

Something wakes me. I can't quite place it. According to the clock, it's a few minutes after midnight. Maryanne, making her usual grunts and squeaks, sleeps in her crib. I hear the television in the living room. Fred wanted to watch the primary results. I walk into the room to see who won.

"They shot him," a somber-faced Fred says before I can speak.

"Who?"

"Robert Kennedy. He won the primary, gave a speech, and they shot him."

"Who shot him?"

"The police nabbed a suspect and hustled him out."

Bewildered, Fred and I watch the news unfold on the screen. Two months ago, almost to the day, it was Martin Luther King Jr. It feels as if the earth spins out of control.

Vietnam

Here, today, we receive news that Senator Robert Kennedy is dead. I've never felt so helpless in all my life. I'm fed up with the filth and the stench of death here and at home. Somehow, I feel safer here.

-26-

In the Roots

Vietnam

I'm assigned to fly with Mister Overton, a new arrival. We're on our way to Kontum with a new crew to move supplies for firebase Mile High. Surveillance devices picked up information that indicates a marshaling of NVA on surrounding ridges. Overton flies the helicopter from Phu Hiep to Kontum.

"You're wearing a .38 pistol, Mister Overton."

"I prefer the lighter weight."

"Ah. Well, most of us are into stopping power."

He looks at my M2. "I sort of figured that. We'll see how it goes."

We take on fuel and start on our sortie sheet. The log pad gives us a load of C-rations and ammo to deliver to Mile High just before lunch. We take sporadic ground fire going in and out.

Next, we take a sling load of howitzer shells. The ground fire is more intense, the NVA telling us they like our route in and out of Mile High. The adage, "Third time's the charm," comes to mind.

We take on fuel for the third trip and eat our C-rations inside our Chinook, out of the sun.

"Listen up," I start. "The ground fire is increasing. I'll try to find a new way into Mile High. If we fly in the same way, I think it might get pretty warm."

"What other route is there?" Overton asks.

"Rather than staying high, in the center of the valley, we can fly a little south of our last route, come up on the treetops. There's a small clearing over there we can use to align ourselves with Mile High's heliport." I stop and light a cigarette. "Questions? Comments?"

Everyone is quiet.

"Okay. Let's get ready."

A Jeep drives alongside our Chinook and stops. A major comes onto the aircraft ramp. "Who's in charge?"

Everyone points at me, and I introduce myself.

"Mister Weatherill, we've got classified ammo, hot food, and ten replacements for Mile High. Everything goes internal, understand?"

"Yes, Sir."

The classified ammo is fleshette. When fired, they send hundreds of tiny steel arrows out the barrel. The rounds are used in overrun situations.

"Ground fire is increasing. Mile High's expecting mortars," the major says.

It could be a weather forecast: cloudy, expecting rain. But it's a war forecast. We need to get in and out.

The aircraft loaded, we leave the Kontum log pad westbound. The flight is twenty-five minutes, the same time it just took us to eat lunch.

"Overton, tell them we're inbound, please."

"Mile High, Windy Seven Zero is on approach."

"Put it right on the heliport, Windy, and we'll get you unloaded in record time."

"Thank you, Mile High," Overton answers.

As his finger releases his mike button, the jungle releases a fusillade at our Chinook. Our gunners return fire into the canopy. An explosion rocks the ship; the number one engine fire light comes on, and the fire bell assaults our ears. We approach uphill, and it becomes our downfall. We're too heavy to climb at that speed with only one engine.

Only five more seconds to the heliport, but it's not to be. We're going down. We're going in the jungle.

"Weatherill, come right, a hard one-eighty. We can make the clearing," Overton calls.

"Talk to me!"

"Keep coming around! Ninety degrees more, you're looking good! Sixty degrees, you should have it!"

"I've got the clearing!" I yell.

There's just enough room to flare the Chinook and land without rolling. Except for the engine, we seem to be in one piece. We can't believe our luck. Now, we only have to get up to Mile High.

"Overton, shut us down." I begin our survival plan.

"Yes, Sir." He flies into action.

"Chief, have the grunts help you set up a perimeter, fast. I expect we'll have company."

"Done, Sir!" he answers.

"Windy Seven Zero. Windy Seven Zero, Mile High!" the firebase contacts us.

"Mile High, Windy Seven Zero is down. We need gunship cover," I respond.

"Windy Seven Zero, it will take us at least thirty, three-zero minutes to get to you. Do you copy?"

"Thirty minutes; Seven Zero copies." *My God!*

The blades decelerate to a stop and the Chinook settles onto the ground. Jungle sounds replace the whine of the helicopter transmissions. Then, we hear the forecast mortar attack rain on Mile High.

"Our thirty minutes just expired," Overton observes.

Our crew chief runs to the cockpit with a grunt sergeant in tow. "Sir, Sergeant Floyd has some ideas."

"Spit 'em out," I say.

"We need to booby trap the ship, Sir."

"Do it, Sergeant!" I turn my attention to my crew gathered at the companionway. "Get the machine guns and all the ammo you can carry. Get up to the trees, one on each side. Leave room for the rest of us between you."

The gunners turn on their heels and disappear.

"Chief, get our smoke grenades and your M-79 up to the trees," I continue.

"What about the cypher?" the crew chief asks.

"I'll destroy the cypher," I respond.

The cypher is in the radio compartment behind the left pilot seat. On the back of the box is a handle that somehow wipes it clean. I pull the handle and get my rifle. Then, I exit the helicopter and head uphill to our defensive positions.

Sergeant Floyd booby-traps our Chinook and comes uphill to the trees. "Sir, if it blows, it's going to take the fleshette ammo with it. I suggest we defend ourselves with these trees between us and your helicopter."

"You heard the man," I whisper to our group. "Quiet as mice, gentlemen."

At the edges of the clearing, tualang trees reach more than 200 feet overhead. Huge roots jut out like barricades. The uphill side affords a better hiding position. We settle among the massive roots and try to disappear off the face of the earth.

The snap of breaking twigs is almost indiscernible in the din of the attack on Mile High. I look at my watch. We've been on the ground twenty minutes. We hear gunships fire on positions to our north.

As fast as it started, the attack on Mile High ends. The twigs broadcast the approach of NVA soldiers from the north. Then, we hear men at a run. We are as ready as we can be, and we have an advantage: they think we're a crew of five, not a force of fifteen.

Vietnamese voices approach our Chinook. Our trails in the grass going uphill, away from our helicopter, point straight at us.

The enemy sounds stop. My ears strain to hear.

Suddenly, an NVA soldier appears around the root I'm trying to graft myself to and steps on my left boot. I shoot three rounds into his chest. He falls lifeless beside me. A second enemy soldier scrambles over my root and spots his dead comrade. I shoot him, too.

We all open fire from behind our trees and catch eight men retreating through the open field beside our helicopter. Our machine gunners kill them in a crossfire, and we go back into hiding. According to my watch, forty-five minutes have passed. I hug the tree and stand on my tiptoes to peer over the top of my root. I nod to a grunt who's also looking around.

Then, we hear a Huey coming uphill toward us. It hovers above our Chinook and descends below the canopy. When I think the gunship crew is looking in our direction, I wave from the side of the tree, trying to indicate where we're hiding. The left door gunner waves back and gives me a thumbs up. He also motions that he sees the dead NVA before the gunship climbs out of the trees, passes directly overhead, and continues up to Mile High.

We stay well hidden.

Overton crawls around my root and sees the two dead NVA. "You injured?"

"No."

"Dare we try to talk to anybody?"

"They know we're here. I got a thumbs up from the gunship."

"What do you want to do, now?" he asks.

I think about CW3 Burrows' mantra, "Is it secure?" Right now he makes sense. "Wait," I reply.

"Wait?"

"Make a nest and wait."

"Okay." He looks at my M2. "I want one of those."

My watch says we've been in the jungle two hours and thirty-three minutes when the first men from Mile High get to us.

After staying the night on Mile High, we climb down to our Chinook with a crew of mechanics flown in to help. They defuse the helicopter, take delivery of a new engine, and have us ready for flight in a matter of hours. My crew climbs aboard, and we fly the cargo up to Mile High. Then, we deliver the maintenance team to Camp Holloway, refuel and head for Phu Hiep.

Lieutenant Kase meets us at our parking revetment. "We heard you spent another night on a firebase."

"Yeah, we did. They didn't have any scotch, either," I say.

Overton walks over to Kase and me. He doesn't say anything; he simply holds out his hand. We shake to our survival. Then, we head for operations and our debriefing. I have citations to write.

Back in my hooch, I wonder when the nightmare will show up.

Riverside, California: Annie

I'm in line to mail a Father's Day package to Jim.

"Is that what I think it might be? A bespectacled, grandmotherly woman smiles and points to Maryanne's footprints stamped on the brown wrapping paper.

"Yes," I reply.

I don't like to tell people that Jim is in Vietnam. They always ask, "Don't you worry about him?" I always tell them the part where I have confidence that he can take care of himself. They mean well. They don't need to know the rest.

"I have two grandsons over there." The woman smiles again, but dabs her eyes with a tissue.

"God bless," I reply.

How many generations has she seen off to war? I wonder. Do you ever get used to it? It's my turn at the counter.

"What's in the package?" asks the postal clerk.

"Cookies, dried soup, hot chocolate mix, other food, and a tape recording."

"Any weapons?"

I blink in surprise. "Of course not. He's in a war zone. He already has a gun."

A man behind me chuckles.

27

Over the Line

Vietnam

Ben Het and Dak To are back in business, but on a smaller scale. On one of the rare days that Alesti and I fly together, we head north to Dak To.

When we land to refuel, we're met by a captain who needs to coordinate the recovery of one of his long-range patrols. He tells us that the team, positioned to observe movement along a piece of the Ho Chi Minh trail at the Laos-Vietnam frontier, has been recalled. They have observed North Vietnamese regulars filling the area around them.

The weather isn't objectionable. The catch is that the team is moving to avoid discovery. The captain gives us the team's last coordinates, which are well inside the borderline with Laos, a no-fly zone. He says the whole thing should be a cakewalk. I remember my mother saying, "One woman's cake is another woman's calories." Sort of a dieter's Worry Line.

We takeoff, head west and cross over Ben Het, about five kilometers inside Vietnam, where Vietnam, Cambodia and Laos form a T.

"I don't like this," I say as we leave Vietnam behind and my Worry Line falls onto the border.

"Well, we can't wait for them to walk to Ben Het." Alesti scans the sky. "We're supposed to get a gun team. Anybody see any Hueys?"

"Not yet," Wellish and Jacaby answer.

"Let me see if I can get the patrol," Alesti says. "David, David, this is Windy Nine, over!"

"Windy Nine, this is David," the patrol answers.

"Windy Nine is inbound, David."

"Windy Nine, David will pop smoke when we see you." David's smoke signal will help us locate them.

Alesti looks at his watch and then back outside. "David, do you hear our rotor noise?"

"David hears you." David's voice is almost a whisper.

"Something's changed," I say.

"Something has definitely changed," Alesti agrees.

We fly across a ridge and a small river, and see a wisp of purple smoke rising from the timber.

"Purple smoke, Windy." David whispers.

Purple smoke clouds pop up all along the ridge and down the sloping ground.

"Jesus!" Alesti says, then keys the radio, "David, we will call your smoke. Do not call your smoke. I repeat, do not call your smoke."

"Windy, we're on the move. Sorry, man." Small arms fire pops like static in the radio. "We're going to have to make an LZ. Give us a couple minutes."

"Keep moving, David. When you stop, pop two smokes and we will call them."

"David has popped smoke!"

The gun fire stops for the moment.

"Yellow, yellow!" Alesti calls. Double smokes of all combinations drift upward all over the ridge and the valley below.

"That's us, Windy."

"We'll give you cover. Keep moving! Keep moving!" We urge them.

"Roger that!"

We move up the ridge and see NVA running among the trees. Jacaby and Wellish commence firing, and Steele launches M-79 rounds out Wellish's gun port. The long range patrol rushes toward an opening in the canopy.

"Windy, we'll blow a few trees so you can get in. We have two men setting det-cord. Four of us are covering."

"Roger, David." We go downslope, and then back up the ridge. The number of NVA increases. We continue shooting.

"Windy, we've blown four trees. It's all the det-cord we had left," David tells us.

I head straight for the opening, drop in the hole, and we settle on the limbs of the downed trees. The patrol climbs over the limbs, toward the rear of the helicopter. Steele jumps off the ramp, grabs two wounded men and pushes them into the Chinook. The wounded men pull themselves to the gun ports and open fire with Jacaby and Wellish. Gunfire intensifies from all sides, closing us in a vise. The NVA appear at the edges of the clearing and Alesti opens fire from his window.

"Everyone's aboard, Sir! Everyone's aboard!"

I pull pitch and start up. The rotor wash from the blades creates enough of a maelstrom to allow us the seconds we need to begin our escape. Then, there's an explosion on the right side of the little LZ, then, one on the left, then another and another.

"Hey, Windy, Gun Lead! Depart straight out! We got your flanks and your six big boy!" The gunships are here.

"Straight ahead, roger."

"Sorry, we're late."

"You're right on time, Lead," Alesti answers.

We fly straight west, gaining speed as we hug the tops of the trees for cover. We break south, then east and head at flank speed for the border. We do not want to get caught on this side. Why does fleeing always seem to take so long?

"We're right behind you, Windy," Gun Lead says. "Hurry. Go fast."

"This is it," I say. We can only wish for more speed.

"It'll do then. Again, sorry we were late."

"Buy us a drink someday."

"You're on."

*   *   *

Do I believe in angels?

Do I believe in angels....

It is time displaced, when you're behind and can't catch up. You drive onto black ice before you can slow down. You put the boat engine in reverse and it quits coming into the dock. You fly into the earth because there is not enough air in front of you to avoid your doom. Little points of no return can be big points of no return if you die.

I read, I study, I think, I pray, I do good and I do bad. I'm not clairvoyant. I don't carry a talisman or a relic. I have a St. Christopher medal in my footlocker. I don't wear it because I don't want to yell at it if it doesn't protect what it's supposed to protect; not do what it's supposed to do.

There are times when I can't explain the simplest of happenings. How can the barrel be pointed at me and the bullet miss?

I'm not superstitious. If I feared all the things that scare me, I would never leave my hooch. Thirteen is not my favorite number, but neither is seven. I seem to like the color yellow. I used to like green, but it's become monotonous. I have memories of nuns beating on my knuckles. I ask questions and listen. In church, I'm sure I sit among other sinners.

Now, I'm in a war zone and death is everywhere. Their dead and our dead keep me from going to church. Rational life has disappeared. I leave the organized flock. I synthesize my position for my sanity: I believe in duty and America and angels.

Father Thomas shows up at the heliport where we are refueling. "Mister Weatherill, I want you to take me to the firebase."

"Father Thomas, are you crazy? You know the standing order. You'll have to wait until the battle's over."

"You and I have talked about the complexity of religion in war. I have no martyr's death wish, Mister Weatherill. I know I can do good out there."

"People are dying out there."

"I rest my case."

"Okay, Father, the only thing they can do to me is more of this. But what about you; have you thought what they'll do to you?"

"I refuse to be a hypocrite."

"Father, it's your ass. But when you wind up in hell, you make sure you tell them I'm the one who flew you there."

"Thank you, Mister Weatherill."

Yes, I believe in angels.

28

Resupplies and Goodbyes

Vietnam

The Army installed in some of our helicopters a system of navigation known as Decca. It's a beautiful, low frequency navigation system with four delicate instrument bodies feeding information to a rectangular box mounted between the pilots in the cockpit.

The box contains a rolled chart. A stylus is mounted to the top of the map box; the helicopter is the end of the stylus. The chart moves with the movement of the helicopter. When we leave the planet, the instruments follow our movement and keep us located in reference to the earth's surface. As the helicopter flies, the box unrolls a chart of the countryside. If the stylus says we're flying through hell, we can look outside and see flames.

The Decca works beautifully until the little, sterile, thermally-sealed units that refine information meet ultra-fine Vietnam clays. After that, if the Decca says we're landing on the main runway at Ban Me Thout, we can expect anything from a commissary parking lot to a lunar landscape.

Captain Dodge first discovers that the Decca isn't up to snuff while landing in coastal fog at Nha Trang. His instruments show him in the center of the airfield runway, when he's actually on the grass outside the PX. He shuts down his helicopter, goes in the exchange, and buys out their stock of girlie magazines. He's himself again. He has a new purpose. He becomes elusive, avoids drinks and conversation at our little bar. When he finally surfaces, he walks into the morning operations briefing, grinning like he's going home early.

"Let's get this thing started," Major Black, our new operations officer orders.

We settle in our chairs.

"As we all know," Black continues, "the Decca is a good idea. However, some of you have been pouring food, sweat, and powered clay all over the sensitive instruments. And in case any of you missed it, Captain Dodge almost mated his Chinook with the Nha Trang PX a couple weeks ago. This incident, along with a few other less serious, caused us to stop using the Decca for primary navigation. Do not use it, understood?"

No one answers.

"Good. Captain Dodge, you have something to say?"

Dodge walks to the front of the briefing room. He pauses, looking at us for a moment. "We're going to help the Koreans today. More resupply. Some of you will stay over at Phan Rang for a few days. I want to say goodbye to all of you. If you're going south, I'll be gone before you get back. I can't say I've enjoyed the war, but I've enjoyed knowing all of you. We helped each other stay alive, and I'm grateful for that.

"I'm going to battalion for a few days, and then I'm out of here. As Bob Hope says, 'thanks for the memories.'"

He goes from man to man shaking hands and sits down.

The sortie board has Alesti, Travis, Kase and me going south. This is exasperating. Dodge is our big brother, teacher, mentor, and friend. We figured one more mission, a party, and our goodbyes. Now, we're coming up dry. How do you shake hands with someone and never see him again? This God forsaken place, every day there's something new. I should have stayed in bed.

Seven months of staying alive with Dodge, and now to

feel so cheated out of the last few days. Well, bless him; he spent his life paying for his year one day at a time and made a couple days' interest.

So, we leave and head south for Phan Rang. The day is clear. It's warm at our 3,000-foot cruising altitude, and our windows are open. As we proceed south along the Vietnamese coast, we talk occasionally to some of the control zones we pass for flight identification and flight plan updates.

"I was looking forward to putting his shit in the Jeep," Travis says.

"So was I."

"Lieutenant Kase is due out soon, too," Travis adds.

"End of the month, unless they pull him early." I look at our fuel gauges. Based on their quantity, we're close to our destination.

"Let's get on with it, then," Travis says, pushing his ADF switch on, filling his helmet with music.

After a while, we land and refuel at the coastal base at Phan Rang. Then, we head to the logistics pad for the Korean sorties. It turns into a blivet kind of day. We hook up a double load and head west for firebase Consort, about twenty-five kilometers inland. The beauty of the day is calming with home sounds from Armed Forces Radio in our ears. The trip is quick, and we turn on the approach to Consort.

"Windy Four Seven, we want the first blivet in the hole at the north end of the base," the Korean controller says.

"And the second?" Travis asks.

"The second at the south end."

"Okay, Consort," Travis answers.

I slow the Chinook and come to a hover.

"Forward fifteen," Steele directs. "Forward five. We're good. Stop."

I hover.

"Down ten ... five ... one. On the ground. Down five more and we'll unhook."

As the first sling unhooks, a mortar round explodes at the south end of the firebase. A second mortar lands next to the first.

"First blivet unhooked, Sir. Clear to come up," Steele announces.

The firebase comes alive. Soldiers scamper for their firing positions.

"Windy, Windy," Consort calls, "depart immediately. Depart immediately!"

We lift, still carrying the second blivet, back into the sky and flee to the east.

Consort opens fire on the suspected mortar position. Cannon shells chew up the side of a ridge.

"You want to be a bomber?" Travis asks.

"Elaborate, please." I'm climbing to get away from the fight.

"We drop our blivet on the mortar position and the Koreans fire at it. Sorta like homemade napalm, only plain diesel."

"Brilliant, Travis."

"Consort, Windy Four Seven, over," Travis calls.

The mortar fire moves closer and closer to the cannon pits.

"Windy Four Seven, Consort, go ahead."

"We can drop this blivet on the mortar position. You can fire for effect, maybe burn them out."

"Standby."

We know the idea is being passed on to be assessed and if they agree, the cannon fire will be coordinated. From our high altitude, we see two other cannons rotate toward the suspected mortar position. The idea must be a hit.

"Windy Four Seven, begin your attack, please," Consort directs.

So, we become a bomber. I turn toward the ridge and accelerate to full speed. We take ground fire. Jacaby and Wellish open up with their machine guns to keep the VC heads down. We release the blivet when we are 200 feet above the ridge and transfer all our energy into altitude. Consort opens fire.

Instead of high explosive rounds, the first two salvos from the firebase are white phosphorus. The side of the ridge becomes a white and yellow inferno.

"Windy Four Seven, Consort, over."

"Four Seven, go ahead," Travis answers.

"We'll assess the problem and call through the log pad when it's safe for your return."

"Roger, Consort," Travis answers. "We'll wait."

Our bombing mission complete, we turn east toward the South China Sea and lunch at Phan Rang. As we approach the log pad we see Alesti and Kase's Chinook parked at the east side of the pad. We land and park behind them, then help our crew check oil and hydraulic fluid levels and the general condition of our Chinook. This exercise takes about twenty minutes. We do it every four hours. It's a stay-alive ritual; helicopter care and feeding. When we finish, we eat C-rations in the shade of Alesti's ship.

Alesti deliberates where he should go on R&R.

"I'd go to Australia if I could do it again," Kase offers. "I wasted my time and money seeing my wife in Hawaii."

"How come?" Alesti asks, putting his last spoonful of ham and lima beans in his mouth.

"Because the women have round eyes, and they speak English."

Alesti swallows. "That's not enough."

"It would be easy to find a virgin."

"I don't want a virgin."

Travis looks up from an unsuccessful nap. "You ought to send your ex-wife a bomb, Lieutenant. She's making you stranger by the day."

"The divorce papers are still in the mail, Travis." Kase smiles.

Alesti opens his cookie tin. "Virgins are a pain in the ass. They don't know what to do or how to do it. You're supposed to teach them and make them want you at the same time—just a plain pain. I'm thinking Hong Kong." Alesti offers his cookies, but no one seems interested in them or his Hong Kong comment.

"Maybe Fran can set you up with one of the Evac nurses, Lieutenant," I suggest. "It would help us all."

Alesti leans on an elbow. "Listen, Lieutenant, I'll give you some of the magazines Captain Dodge left me. They'll help you see the rest of the picture. Hong Kong. Anyone?"

"Look, Alesti, I'll give you the money for the trip if you'll go kill my wife."

"Nice try, but you're going to be home in the good old U.S.A. at the end of the month. Do it yourself. I'm going to Hong Kong. Besides, murder's a mortal sin; you only get to go to hell."

"Why Hong Kong?" Travis asks.

"Because you can buy women for anything, anytime, anywhere," Alesti answers.

"Bangkok is the same," Travis says. "It only takes money."

Kase stands up and dusts himself off. "You guys are perverts," he says.

We finish our lunch, climb back in our helicopters, and fly back into war.

Riverside, California: Annie

Except for the usual agitators, most people on campus haven't been demonstrating or draft card burning. There has been some concern about lifting draft deferments for graduate students, but the loudest protests come from the professors who fear they won't have anyone to correct papers and work as teaching assistants.

There's got to be something wrong in the world that every generation has to fight in a war. I just can't understand war. I don't have a whole lot of faith that any war will end all wars because there's something basic to war and the human race.

Now, Laos is beginning to cry that the communists are trying to take over. I'd like to tell them that if it bothers them so much, they ought to do something about it besides complain. The men who have infiltrated through their country have killed a lot of Americans, and they didn't seem to be too concerned when it was our loss.

Vietnam

Alesti returns from Hong Kong the day before Lieutenant Kase is to take the Big Bird back to America.

"I'm afraid to go home," Kase offers, halfway inside a bottle of gin.

"Lieutenant, you need to settle up with that woman. You need to move on," Alesti says. He pulls two boxes out from under his cot and places them on his bed.

Travis shakes his head. "Don't do anything stupid, okay? There are too many good women out there."

Alesti opens the top box, extracts a tailored silk suit, and holds it against his chest. "What do you think?"

"Very nice," I answer. "Where do you wear something that pretty?"

"At the bars, the nightclubs. Women will love them."

"Expensive?" Travis asks.

"Yes." Alesti returns the suit to its box and opens the other box. "Yeah, they'll love them," he says to himself.

Kase lights a cigarette. He smokes slowly. His quiet, drooping eyes say he's ready to call it a night. "You know what?" He looks up at all of us. "You guys have been the best." Then, he tips over on his side, asleep.

Alesti takes the cigarette from his hand. "I don't think he understands that he's headed home tomorrow."

I recover the gin. "I don't think he's packed, either."

Travis, Alesti, and I go to Kase's hooch and discover Isaac's painting. It has Kase on the top of a rise, a U.S. flag on a short staff beside him. He has one foot on a rock and aims the pistol in his hand at infinity. We pack his stuff, line it all up by his bunk, and then carry him from our hooch to his bed and tuck him in.

"God looks after puppies and drunks," Travis proclaims.

"So do angels," I add.

We walk to our little bar and hang Lieutenant Kase's portrait on the wall next to the one of Captain Dodge.

PART 9

JULY 1968

143 DAYS TO GO

29

Recovery

Vietnam

Ban Me Thout sits in the southern third of the Central Highlands. With miles of rubber plantations, the highland plains provide perfect infiltration routes.

We bring firebases from around Pleiku south to Ban Me Thout. This is no easy feat, with ninety-mile legs in helicopters so heavy that once in the air 90 knots is as fast as they can go. Anything past that, the sling load, or the helicopter, tries to go wild. The move is into day five, and boredom in the cockpit causes complacency.

We set up some ground rules: First, the guy flying has to fly the round trip; Second, naps are allowed as long as we disable the helicopter's stability system so the flying pilot will stay awake—it's like standing on an inner tube in a swimming pool; Third, the non-flying pilot can do anything he wants—eat, sleep, listen to Armed Forces Radio, take pictures, tell jokes, whatever; Fourth, a door gunner is assigned the duty of chef for a round trip.

On the Chinook our regular 115v outlets can easily handle a coffee pot, electric skillet, razor or toaster. Under a forward fold-up seat, we keep some amenities of life in a wooden box. We carry potable water, coffee, cigarettes, assorted dried foods, C-rations, and sometimes cookies from home. Mysteriously, eggs and different meats find their way into our ship's pantry. It's amazing what a little creativity with your basic C-rations produces.

Somewhere in the days of tedium, our ship is called off the long-haul mission. I'm flying with Overton, gunners Jacaby and Wellish and crew chief Steele. We land at the refueling pad at Ban Me Thout East Airfield and top off the Chinook. Then, we reposition to the Special Forces log pad. Two Special Forces sergeants arrive beside the helicopter in a Jeep. While we talk, the Chinook is loaded with cannon shells.

"No sling load?" I ask.

"No, Sir, this stuff's fleshettes. It's classified ammo. We can only transport it internal."

"Where are we going with it?"

"Well, northwest of here, about forty-five minutes."

"If my memory serves me correctly, Sergeant, that's Cambodia."

"Well, yes, Sir, you can see Cambodia from there. But, it's not Cambodia."

"Okay, Sergeant, let's get it over with." Then, I call the crew out and brief them on what to expect.

It's an easy flight the first fifteen minutes, until we hit fog. Below us, a gray carpet covers everything as far northwest as we can see toward our destination. We use time, distance, heading and airspeed to dead reckon to the rendezvous with the Special Forces outpost. Normally, topography is also a big help, but the only surface feature under us now is a smooth layer of fog.

At the end of the timeline, we call on our FM radio. "Otis, Otis, this is Windy Seven Zero, over."

No response.

"Otis, Otis, this is Windy Seven Zero, over," Overton calls again.

"Windy Seven Zero, this is Otis. We hear your helicopter, but we don't see you. Too much fog, over."

"Otis, key your mike for thirty seconds and we'll home in on your signal. After thirty seconds, un-key your mike, and listen for us," Overton instructs.

"Okay, Windy, key for thirty seconds starts now," Otis responds.

We use our bearing indicator to direct us to the ground position. The FM homing has only one problem: unless the people on the ground tell you, or you see them, you don't know when you fly over them. The thirty seconds end and our homing needle dies.

"Otis, have we passed your position?" Overton asks.

"You are overhead now."

I slow the helicopter to 50 knots. "Okay, everybody, let's find them," I say to the crew.

"Otis, can you fire a flare straight up?"

"One minute, Windy."

I reverse our course using heading references and turn to the rotor wash line lying on the top of the fog. The straight line of the sinking rotor wash brings us back to Otis.

"Flare launched," Otis says.

"Flare in sight," Overton acknowledges.

We fly a tight circle around the point where the flare has come up out of the fog and slow to a hover. All our rotor wash now goes straight down.

"I see them," Steele calls from Wellish's gun port.

"I got 'em, too," Jacaby calls.

We hover, blowing a Chinook-size hole in the fog. It's taking too long. We're a big, noisy target, and we're not moving. Finally, I see the heliport through the chin bubble.

"I've got the heliport. We're landing. Keep us clear," I announce to the crew.

We are unloaded and in flight for Ban Me Thout in twenty minutes. The fog now becomes our friend, hiding our departure. We stay the night in Ban Me Thout.

The next day, while delivering hot rations to an encampment west of the city, we get news over the air-net that a Huey has been shot down to the northwest.

"You suppose they were over at Otis?" Overton questions.

"Windy Seven Zero, Ban Me Thout Control," comes over the radio.

"Windy Seven Zero, go ahead, Control,"

"This is a recall. You are to return to the Special Forces log pad, immediately."

"Windy Seven Zero, roger. ETA eleven minutes, over," we respond.

"Eleven minutes, roger," Control acknowledges.

I look around and find my Worry Line coiled on the aircraft floor between the pilot seats. Overton lands us at the Special Forces log pad. A fuel truck comes alongside to top off our fuel tanks while the log pad crew unloads our internal cargo. I climb off the helicopter and ride to the log pad operations room.

"That your bird?" asks a Special Forces captain standing inside the door.

"Yes, Sir, it is."

"You take the mission to Otis yesterday?"

"I did," I look at his name on his fatigue jacket, "Captain Nelson. I'm Mister Weatherill."

"Well, Mister Weatherill, we lost a Huey a couple miles from Otis. The recovery team is in position to extract the Huey except ..." He stops and chews on his thoughts a few seconds. "Plain and simple, things have gone to shit."

"Define shit for me, Captain Nelson."

"The crew is lost. We need to recover the bodies and the recovery team."

"And?"

"And, they're surrounded. You need to extract them."

"The fog still there?" I ask.

"Not as bad as yesterday."

This is not necessarily good news.

"Gun cover?"

"They'll be orbiting, waiting for your directions," Captain Nelson answers. "It's one of my recovery teams. I'd like to go with you, if that's acceptable."

"It may only be one way, Captain. Stay, go, you decide. Any help is welcome." We walk together to the ship for a talk. The news about our next sortie is sobering to everyone. We stand in the cargo compartment, looking at each other, sizing up our fates. No one says anything; not one question or quip. After introductions of the rest of the crew and Captain Nelson, we move to our duty stations to get under way.

"We're going to be close on fuel," Overton says.

"I agree. Steele, you hear that?"

"Yes, Mister Weatherill."

It's my turn to fly. Halfway to the recovery site, the gun team, a couple of Huey gunships, from Ban Me Thout joins us.

"Windy Seven Zero, Gun Lead," the lead gunship radios us.

"Go ahead, Gun Lead," Overton says.

"We'll orbit south and await your call."

"Gun Lead, if we make more noise, rather than less, maybe they won't all move to welcome us, if you get my drift."

"I get the idea. We'll stay east and fly north and south of your hover. Spread out the sound."

The trip is too quick. My mind plays so many scenarios; it has taken time with it.

"Recovery Boss, Windy Seven Zero," Overton calls.

"I'll key for homing, Windy," and his voice ends.

We follow the FM homing signal. Recovery talks us in the last kilometer, and we slow as we approach.

We come to a hover, and Wellish sees someone in the trees. "Eleven o'clock low, Mister Weatherill."

"I've got him." I'm expecting to see a hole in the trees where the Huey crashed, but there's nothing visible. They were swallowed by the jungle, too.

Our rotor wash blows loose pieces of jungle canopy in every direction. The recovery man is wedged against the tree trunk. Four hand grenades hang across his chest. His rifle is in one hand and he points straight down with the other.

"Keep us out of the trees," I direct Overton. "Steele, you see the ground?"

"Yes, Sir, forward ten, please ... five ... stop. Hover here. Line out?"

"Line out."

With our helicopter nested in the treetops, we let out 220 feet of line, and the upload begins. One by one, the recovery team from Otis sends up the body bags holding the remains of the four Huey crew members.

Captain Nelson helps Steele lay the body bags side by side near the aft ramp. We've hovered thirty-five minutes.

Then, we begin to hoist the recovery team through the cargo hook hole and curse at how slowly it seems to go. Seventy minutes into the extraction, we have four of the seven men on board.

"Windy Seven Zero, Recovery Boss."

"Windy," Overton answers.

"They're coming."

We hear rifle reports in the background of his transmission. The VC broadcast their fire, chumming with bullets. The team doesn't fire back.

"Clamp on, we'll take you both at once."

"We are clamped on. Bring us up and we'll grab our tree hugger."

"Expect ground fire, men. Remember, the recovery team is on the line," Overton says to our gunners.

"Bring them up; everybody stay sharp," I say. We can't begin our climb out of our hover hole until everyone is clear of the trees.

"We're reeling in," Steele says.

Then the real shooting starts.

"Hold, Mister Weatherill."

I steady our hover. "What's happening, Steele?"

"The man in the tree is hooking onto the line. He's dropping his grenades."

The tick of bullets hitting the helicopter increases with each passing second.

"Gun Lead, strafe both sides! We have three recovery members on the line! Increasing ground fire!" Overton says into his microphone.

"Lead is rolling in left side."

"Gun Two, right side."

We reel the three recovery men up through the maze of tree limbs as the gun team pours rockets and thousands of rounds into the jungle. White phosphorus rockets seem to work the best to reduce the volume of ground fire.

"Recovery team is clear of the trees. Clear! Clear!" Steele calls out.

I climb straight up. Once above the gun team, I pedal turn to the heading for Ban Me Thout and begin a slow acceleration. We need to get the three men dangling below us away from the ground fire. Captain Nelson helps pull the last men through the Chinook's hook well.

"Recovery team is aboard," Steele informs. "One just died. Two are wounded. Captain Nelson and the others are working on them."

"Windy Seven Zero, Gun Lead."

"Windy Seven Zero," Overton answers.

"How'd we do?" Gun Lead asks.

"We wouldn't have made it without you," Overton says.

"What about the recovery team?"

"One dead, two wounded," Overton replies.

"God bless them."

"Indeed."

30

Hawaii Is to the East

Vietnam

My mind flashes like a neon sign: Hawaii. Annie. Hawaii. Annie. Everything takes its time, but goes along, on schedule. I'm not dead, and the island is right over there to the east, just out of reach. With one more night to go, I can't sleep.

Miller bangs on the hooch door and sticks his head inside. "Card game tonight. Table stakes $100; maximum bet $25; Blackjack. Interested?"

It's the answer to my anxious insomnia.

"Absolutely," I say and follow Miller to our officers' bar.

Miller and I sit opposite each other. Alesti is at my right. Seated to my left is a Huey pilot.

Sitting between Miller and the Huey pilot is a lieutenant from battalion operations. He was out for a stroll and got lost enough to find his way to our small bar. He says cards are not his strong suit. We write a short list of hit or hold pairings to help him determine if he should take a card or stay. The list is an excuse not to be responsible for his loses.

I'm winning and send money to the bar, repaying my friends for their protection. A glass of whiskey is the same as a couple of cigarettes, maybe a bar of soap or a good call coming out of an LZ. Whiskey is currency. It's its own scrip.

The lieutenant's beginner's luck eventually gets on the Huey pilot's nerves. Out of the blue, the pilot gets to his feet and jams what's left of his money in his pocket. "Damn it all," he says in disgust. He looks at us as if he wants to say something more, but he doesn't. He turns to the door and stomps out. All mouths hang open.

"We've got an empty seat," Miller offers those standing at the bar.

A stranger, a lieutenant colonel, looks our way. At Miller's offer, he gets up from the bar, comes to the table and pulls out a chair. We meet our new commanding officer.

*   *   *

At last, I catch a Herc that takes me to Cam Ranh Bay, where I catch a plane painted in civilian colors. That plane takes me to Hawaii—America, at least a piece of it.

In Hawaii, I join a line of men, and we climb on buses that take us to downtown Honolulu. I look out the bus window like a kid. We stop, the bus doors open, and we file out. This is unlike the Army. Nobody tells us what we're supposed to do.

We walk between two rows of beautiful women. Everyone is looking for someone. In the excitement, they all look alike. An arm reaches out and snags me. I've walked right past Annie. We embrace, stopping just before our bones break.

Once we're together, the Army decides to talk to us. No one can concentrate on anything beyond the person in the next seat. When whatever they said is over, I hail a taxi and we're off. I pay for our ride, and we hustle into the hotel and up to the registration desk.

"I'm sorry, Sir, but your room isn't ready, yet," the registration clerk says.

"But I reserved this room two months ago."

"I'm sorry, housekeeping hasn't released it. Please, step into the bar. We'll call you in just a few minutes."

After two drinks, we hear a page and return to the front desk. A guy built like a small Sumo wrestler stands by our two bags. I reach for them, but he stops me.

"Compliments of the house, Sir," the porter says and picks up the bags He escorts us to the elevator and pushes a button. At our room, he unlocks the door and walks in. He turns on a light and puts the bags down at the foot of the bed. Then, he just stands there.

I reach in my pocket, fumble for some quarters and pile the coins in the guy's outstretched hand.

The porter stops halfway to the door and looks in his palm, turns around with a disgusted look on his face, and utters something in Hawaiian that ends with a spitting sound. He throws the coins on the floor and tromps out of our room, slamming the door.

I instinctively reach where my pistol should be. I'm shaking. Money feels strange. In Vietnam we use military scrip, which is paper. Even coins are paper. After eight months using military scrip for currency, a nickel feels the same as a quarter. I laugh, but it's a bitter start.

From that moment, the only thing Annie and I spend at the hotel is time, and then only when necessary. We rent a motorcycle, explore the island, skip the war memorials, lie in the sand and in each other's arms.

Then, it's over.

Just like that.

Eight months of war that seems like eight years of waiting for seven days that pass in the blink of an eye.

PART 10
AUGUST 1968
112 DAYS TO GO

31

Two Head Home

Vietnam

I'm on the edge of my cot, head down, crying. A blue line of smoke rises from the cigarette between my fingers.

The hooch door slams behind Alesti as he walks in. He stops in his tracks and calls for Travis.

"What's the matter?" Alesti asks.

Travis steps through the hole in the wall and stands at my shoulder.

"Robert Wearman is dead," I say.

Alesti drops his helmet and body armor on his cot and takes a bottle of scotch from his locker. Travis lights a cigarette and trades it for the stub hanging in my fingers. He gives Alesti a baffled look.

"Wearman and Weatherill trained together during Chinook transition," Alesti explains.

"I'm sorry," Travis says.

"Short final for fuel," I say. "It came apart in flight. In air, dammit. Gone. Just like that." I swallow some scotch. "The aft pylon came off. The rest of the helicopter hit the ground and exploded."

Alesti puts his hand on my shoulder. "It happens."

"I feel like a hypocrite," I say.

"What do you mean?" Travis asks.

"I haven't cried for any of the others."

"Look," Alesti starts, "we'll have time for all that when we get back. We'll have plenty of help dealing with it, too. Some tears are okay. The dam leaks every now and then."

Travis answers a knock at the door.

"Hello, Mister Travis," Corporal Jacaby begins. "If it's not a good time, ... well, I won't have any other time. It's just that I'm going home in the morning. I wanted to say goodbye to you and Mister Alesti and Mister Weatherill."

"Come in, Jacaby," I call. How many times has his machine gun saved our lives? It's a number I don't care to know.

"How about a whiskey?" Alesti offers.

"Well, Sir. Yes, Sir, I'd like that."

Jacaby takes the drink and swallows it whole.

Alesti pours another. "You're headed home, huh?"

"Yes, in the morning."

I get up. It feels good to stand. "Congratulations," I say offering my hand.

"Thank you, Sir."

Alesti follows, shaking hands. He takes Jacaby's empty glass, refills it, and hands it back. "Thank you for your protection," Alesti says, clinking glasses.

Travis and I step close and clink glasses, too. "Here, here," Travis offers.

"I didn't mean to interrupt, Sir," Jacaby says, noticing my eyes.

"You're not interrupting. It's been a hard day; I lost a friend."

"Well, I just needed to say goodbye."

"Thanks for coming," Alesti says.

"Well, I'm off then. I'm real sorry about your friend, Mister Weatherill."

My mouth becomes cotton. "Well, at least you're both going home," I manage to say.

Short on Pilots, Long on War

Vietnam

Our C.O. drinks from his coffee cup, sets it down, and starts the briefing. "We've got something big coming down. We're going back to Ban Me Thout. Apparently we have an infiltration problem over there. Battalion informed me not to expect any replacements for quite a while. Sorry. We've got sixteen Chinooks, and we're committed to launch seven a day. We'll be down to eighteen pilots this month after all the pilots rotating stateside have left. Sleep when you can, eat when you can. With nobody getting shot, you can expect a day off once a week.

"We'll live in the transient hooches with everybody else. So, try to find some berthing together so we don't have to look all over hell to find you. Captain Dodge left something to help ward off the boredom. Any questions?"

There are none; there never are for the C.O.

We stand at attention, and he leaves the room. Then, Major Black hands each crew a Decca roll, the charts we aren't supposed to use.

"What's up, Sir?" Styki asks.

"Just set these babies up as usual. You'll see," he answers.

We leave the heliport in random sequence and varied initial headings on our way to Ban Me Thout with an open-end contract. The beauty of the day lightens the mood as we pass the end of the compound, turn west and fly back into our war. We see farmers using oxen to work their fields and children everywhere, running along the paddy dikes. We overlook dozens of bomb craters, farm houses lying in rubble, new graves in the ancient cemetery.

The cemetery strikes a nerve—tomb slabs moving, people emerging from graves, death out my window, and life at its most basic: them or me. My mind recalls one carpenter making a child's coffin, his cohort fashioning our automatic pistols. I shake my head and tune the ADF to Armed Forces Radio. My ears flood with music I remember from high school. Something slips in my mind. "Americans first," I mutter.

The Decca roll begins. The mountains are deep green, the paddies light green. A knee rises in the center of the chart. A triangle, the thigh on one side the shin on the other, pushes the mountains and paddies aside. Toward the left edge of the chart, the points of two breasts unfurl. Then, nude after nude, all mixed together, unroll. What a flight of wonder.

"Dodge has attained immortality," someone radios.

"Here, here," another agrees.

As we approach Ban Me Thout, we see thunderstorms rolling on the western horizon and the earth blanketed by low clouds. By afternoon, the clouds will tower more than 40,000 feet. The verdant plains covered with rubber plantations will gladly accept the water. Ah, the tropics.

Travis and I land and refuel. A Jeep with three Special Forces guys shows up, followed by a couple three-quarter ton trucks. As we fuel, a dozen men fill us with 105 mm ammo.

"Refueling complete," Steele calls through the intercom. "Hoses are all clear. Say, Sir, we got fleshettes back here, again. Is there something we should know about?"

"That infiltration rumor must be true," Travis speculates. "Stand by, Steele."

The head Special Forces guy, a sergeant holding a heavily creased map, climbs through the companionway to the cockpit. "This shit needs to go here, Sir." He jabs a finger on the Cambodian border. "I'm going with you."

"You been there before?"

"I live there."

"Unfortunate," Travis observes.

"I'm going to pick up a prisoner and some satchel charges. The guy they got is some NVA lieutenant. Okay to smoke, Sir?"

"Sure, go ahead." Travis nods.

The sergeant lights up and takes a couple drags while he watches the loading from the companionway. "I've been here in the rear for a week. You sure sleep a whole lot better."

Travis looks at the sergeant. "We live on the coast. Anything over one click west is the front to us."

"You know about sleep, then."

"Yeah, we do. We like it and don't get enough."

The sergeant looks around the Chinook. "This is some crate. I bet it gets real hard to hide this thing."

"You plan on using this ammo today, Sergeant?" Travis asks.

"No, Sir, not that I know about."

"You get that, Steele?"

"Yes, Sir, clear to start, Mister Travis."

"Wonderful. Time to go, gentlemen," he says, and starts the Chinook's engines.

"Ramp is up, Mister Travis."

Travis brings the helicopter to a hover. We're off.

The Special Forces sergeant's map has our destination at seventy-five kilometers west, as the crow flies. We will fly 8,000 pounds of fleshette ammo to a Special Forces camp so close to Cambodia we need passports.

Thunderstorms pushing low clouds ahead cover this place we have seen only on a chart. To avoid the cloud-shrouded mountains near the Special Forces camp, we must cross a piece of Cambodia going each way.

"I don't want to whine, but this weather sucks. I'm staying with the low ground. Speak now or forever hold your peace." Travis pushes the nose of the Chinook down, leveling off on the top of the jungle.

"Great minds think alike." I smile at him.

Travis opens his window an inch to draw the cigarette smoke out, then keys his microphone. "We don't shoot first. Everybody got that?"

"Hey, wait a minute, Mister Travis, Sir," Jacaby objects. "I just extended for six months and I don't get to kill today?"

Wellish pounces. "You're a jerk, Jacaby. You were in Cam Ranh Bay, waiting on the jet home, and you extend for this shit? Man, when my turn comes, I'll be out of here so fast the vacuum will suck a Jeep into the South China Sea."

"Fuck you. This is the only place I've ever felt like a part of something. You go live my sucky life in America if you want, shithead."

"The man said we don't shoot first," Steele scolds. "He didn't say 'no killing.' Besides, anybody who extends over here is out of his mind."

"It's okay with me if we don't shoot first," Wellish starts. "Jacaby knows he can't hit anything when he shoots, anyway."

"What's everybody doing on my back?" Jacaby asks. "I'm just patriotic. All of you, get off."

Wellish laughs. "The man never even got to the West Coast. Could of got a quick piece and flown back in a weekend."

"I'm not saying another word. I'm a patriot."

"Well, I guess that's settled then," Travis says.

The Special Forces sergeant sits in the companionway jump seat, chain-smoking along with the rest of us. He tells us about the French girl he fell in love with in Dalat.

We fly on and pick up the call of the radio operator at Bu Krak. "Where you at, Windy?"

"Don't ask."

"Well, if you're coming the way I think you are, keep your eyes open. A Huey took a bunch of hits over there on their way into Bu Prang."

We see nothing as we cross Cambodia and land to unload at Bu Krak. The camp is ready for us.

Steele calls forward from the ramp. "Hey, you know what one of these jokers just told me?"

"No, what?" Travis bites.

"This goddamn place gets mortared every day from two to two-thirty. You know what time it is?"

Travis and I scan the aircraft clocks.

I tap the glass on the clock face. It shows two minutes until two.

The green guys move the heavy ammo boxes like they're pillows. We're almost empty when the first mortar hits. Our sergeant runs up the ramp, pushing his prisoner and dragging a burlap-covered cube.

"Work faster!" Steele urges the Special Forces guys unloading us.

In a minute-long eternity, the unloading is complete. Another mortar lands.

"Clear! Clear!" Steele calls out. "Ramp coming up!"

The sergeant throws the satchel on the helicopter floor, pulls out his pistol and smashes it into the prisoner's head, knocking him out. Then, he bolts to the cockpit. "They said don't go out the valley, don't go north! It's a trap!"

We bring the engines to full power and pedal turn toward a small ridge leading to a mountain two kilometers south of the heliport. We need to climb 2,500 feet immediately. The bottoms of the clouds are 300 feet above the cockpit. We drop the nose of the Chinook so low our rotor heads accelerate like the propellers of a plane.

At 100 knots airspeed, I pull back on the cyclic stick between my legs, pitching up into a furious climb. The rate of climb indicator pegs at 6,000 feet per minute. After our altitude exceeds 5,000 feet, I push the nose over to level out.

Halfway to level, the flight controls lock. They won't budge. We have produced negative gravity. Everything in the helicopter gets light on its feet. The sergeant braces himself against my seatback. The door gunners and crew chief grab onto whatever's handy.

Then it quits. The return of gravity puts hydraulic pressure back in our pumps. We are back in control and high enough to clear anything between us and Ban Me Thout. We stay at 5,000 feet, dial in the Ban Me Thout radio beacon and head northeast. The clouds that were our adversaries going into the Bu Krak camp now protect our escape.

Jacaby, cooks up canned spaghetti and meatballs that taste like they've just been flown in from Rome. He covers the canned pound cake with canned strawberry jelly warmed on the forward transmission. It's exquisite. It's also the only restaurant around.

*   *   *

Duc Lap comes under siege. It's about a thirty-five minute flight southwest of Ban Me Thout and holds a contingent of U.S. Special Forces, Vietnamese forces, and members of various Montagnard tribes, altogether, about 290 soldiers. They've been attacked by about a thousand North Vietnamese Army regulars, with a second thousand-man battalion assisting, and two battalions held in reserve. When we arrive, we find a nightmare of rocket craters, mortar craters, and piles of dead. Our stomachs churn for the men fighting for their lives at Duc Lap.

My crew flies more than thirty-three hours in three days. We live in our helicopter. The flight surgeon comes aboard each time we stop for jet fuel. He sees us, takes our blood pressure, gives us pills, and leaves. We get food, too, if we can eat. We live wide awake for three days and three nights; day, night, sun, stars. Eventually, we feel nothing, remember nothing. The battle rages. We fly and fly and fly.

My mind feels like it's been hit by a rocket. I can't believe Hawaii was only three weeks ago, or was it? And this war, the polar opposite of normal life, the basis, the measuring point, is everything dangerous. The hype of vacation was just a mental subterfuge. What else have I missed? It really doesn't matter now. Goodbye, Hawaii.

We fly over the destruction of Duc Lap and try to reconcile the life lost and the bravery involved in the siege of that very expensive piece of dirt. Loss for attritions sake, some convoluted body count war, cannot become my norm. Kill ratios—three to eight, two to six, five to a hundred—still have American blood on one side.

I only remember two landings in these days; barely an hour of memory. One is when we rescue an Air Force pilot shot down by ground fire near Duc Lap; another is taking on the dead.

I've lost myself to another myself. The Dexedrine amnesia protects me from three days of my life; three days and nights without the slightest clue as to what happened. I've lost a piece of my mind. The flight surgeon took it to keep me alive.

My youth is drowning in the flood of bloody missions my mind absorbs and hides from itself. I can't be so ancient at twenty-two. There has to be a way out, a doorway to the oasis, to recovery.

America ... America ....

PART 11
SEPTEMBER 1968
81 DAYS TO GO

Too Old for Youth

Vietnam

We've been in Ban Me Thout for weeks now, nestled in the Huey pilots' hooches behind the old swimming pool, a sort of concave monument. Life for Huey pilots is difficult. Four gunships and two slicks are lost in the siege for Duc Lap. These are their friends and hooch mates. We drink whiskey, not really talking, all knowing what we're thinking: *What will tomorrow bring?*

"Hey Weatherill," Travis says handing me whiskey, "that jet pilot you rescued crossed over Duc Lap today in a low pass. His sonic boom scared the shit out of us. I guess it was a thank you."

"He's welcome," I say taking the drink.

Alesti drags himself into the hooch and tosses his chicken plate, flak jacket and flight helmet on his cot. He walks over to my cot, takes the glass of whiskey out of my hand, and gulps it down.

Travis gets up, refills Alesti's glass, and gets me another drink. "What gives?" he asks.

"What's happened to time?" Alesti mutters.

Alesti looks like he doesn't want an answer, but Travis gives him one. "Time has only one purpose: it locates us in the flow of life."

Alesti isn't listening.

We're weary from loss and so much danger underfoot. I thought I'd seen Alesti's low point. I'm so naïve. I want to think the future exists for good. I even think I can prove it with some of Travis' snowflakes.

Alesti shakes his head and lights up a cigarette.

"What happened?" I ask.

"You know how many people have been dying out there in the last few weeks? Huh?"

Nobody answers.

Alesti shakes his head again. "Dozens of American lives. Shit, how many hundred VC? For fucking what? I know now my life is stuck in some sort of repeating loop, again, and again, and again. No guarantee you'll make it around the next loop, either."

"Have another drink." I pass the bottle.

"All the pilots. Hell, we drank with those guys last week." Alesti refills his glass and absent mindedly hands the empty bottle back to me.

"We're almost at the end, almost home. Even though they'll probably take us out of here in strait jackets," I offer.

Alesti sits on his cot. "It doesn't matter." He looks at the ceiling; my gaze follows. "Incoming!"

We scramble out of the hooch and race through a shower of mortars to the closest bunker. When the attack ends, we come out of the bunkers and take a deep breath of air. Then we look for our buddies, and our stuff. At one point, after a rocket lands in the empty swimming pool, we all agree there's nothing left worth mortaring.

It's funny that mortars never fall when hooch maids and papasans are on the compound doing domestic chores. As the hooches are destroyed, we have to double up, and we are already guests. The atmosphere smells a lot like it did at Pleiku, Kontum and Dak To in February.

During one of the rocket rains, a man falls through the bunker entrance, crosses my Worry Line, and rolls down the stairs. He bounces off the grenade pit wall and lands on the bunker floor from sheer momentum. Travis and Styki rush to him. A piece of shrapnel protrudes from the chest of his fatigue jacket. His life is gone.

Styki grabs a blanket off a cot and covers our dead companion. For a few minutes, this act seems to lessen the sound of the incoming mortars and rockets. In the faint light of cigarettes, others in the bunker settle against the walls or on cots. Some pull their blankets over their heads. It's as good a way as any to keep from getting splashed by death. There's no property lying near our dead visitor, but we feel his legacy.

Styki lights a smoke. "The cocksucker. Why did he have to die in my bunker?"

Travis reaches over and takes the fresh cigarette out of Styki's hand. "Give it a break, Styki. He's dead."

"The bastard had bad luck. Now it's floating around in here someplace."

My Worry Line is still on the bunker steps. It hadn't caught on the man's feet.

Travis smokes from Styki's cigarette. "You win the asshole award, Styki. How can you possibly be upset?"

"Get off my back, Travis!"

"You're lucky I don't crawl up your ass." Travis elbows me and passes the last half of Styki's cigarette.

The rockets and mortars do not abate; a series of increasing concussions marches our way. A mortar hits outside the bunker door, raining Ban Me Thout dirt across our steps. My Worry Line is still there, still holding.

There's a sudden thump of pressure, and the bunker air becomes dust. Another roar as the dust settles around us. I don't know who notices it first, but suddenly, we're all staring at the nose of a 122 mm rocket that penetrated the roof of our bunker. It did not detonate. Maybe it will. Some are not waiting to find out. Two men run up the dirt strewn bunker steps, cross over my Worry Line, and disappear into the roar of the night.

We hear sobs and prayers from corners of the bunker.

I wonder if I'll ever have good luck again. I'm sure I've just used up most of my life's quota. Is the man underneath the blanket our lucky charm? Is he an angel in disguise? The dead man grates on my mind. Good luck and bad luck, side by side, like letting someone play through. My mind jumps between the mortar in the bunker ceiling and the body on the bunker floor. I feel a burn spot, like someone has put their cigar out on my chest. I light a cigarette and exhale through my nose and mouth, trying to exorcise my ghost.

My mind plays on: Hawaii; Annie, a kiss; a baby daughter I've never met; cookies in a box stamped with the footprints of my child. The cigarette tastes bitter, and I grind the butt into the bunker floor.

It's quiet. The roar is gone, and so is my Worry Line. I leave the bunker with Travis and Styki. Back on the surface, Travis and I shake hands. Styki has left us behind.

The old chief warrants appear in my head. I understand now why they banded together. They had to isolate our inexperience. What would they have done here cloaked in our youth, fifteen, or even twenty years younger?

I'm too old for youth now. I move into the darkest dark and throw up.

Riverside, California: Annie

This morning I go to March Air Force Base to see a doctor for my checkup. It took all month to get an appointment. After the examination, I mention birth control. The doctor says he can't help me because he's a surgeon who came to help with the clinic; I would have to talk to a gynecologist. I asked how I did that, and he said to make an appointment.

I thought my appointment was with a gynecologist, at least that's what I asked for when I called.

34

Goodbye, My Friend

Vietnam

After another long night of mortars and sleeplessness, Alesti's time is up. He's sent to our base at Phu Hiep. He has survived. Our friendship has lasted him long enough.

The C.O. lets me fly back to the coast to help him pack and unwind. When we enter our hooch, Isaac's portrait of Alesti is on his bunk alongside two miniature silk suits.

Alesti picks up the painting. His Chinook carries a sling load with a PX banner trailing behind the cargo net full of goodies.

"Hey, Alesti, what are these?" I hold up one of the suits. "Did you buy these for your nephews?"

"I don't have any nephews," he says to the painting.

"So what are these?"

Something finally clicks. "What the hell?" He rushes over and looks at the suits. "You remember the tailored silk suits I had made in Hong Kong?"

"Yeah, I thought you mailed them stateside."

"No, that would have been too damn easy. This dumb-shit sent them to the local cleaners."

"These are your suits?"

"I can't believe this; I gotta get out of here."

"Hold that thought," I say.

The incident opens the gate to our times, and we start talking; like a teeter-totter bottoming out and pitching you off the top. We stuff everything Alesti owns into a footlocker and a duffel bag, and just as we finish, we pass out on our cots.

The next morning, in a drizzle and a hangover, I help load Alesti's footlocker. He says goodbye to everybody who shows up, five altogether, counting the corporal driving the Jeep.

Alesti and I hug one another like old lovers, and then shake hands. He promises to call Annie when he reaches America.

And he's gone.

I walk over to our officers' club and hang Alesti's picture on the wall next to the others also gone. I take a handful of aspirin and go back to the war.

PART 12
OCTOBER 1968
51 DAYS TO GO

35

Chemical Consequences

Riverside, California: Annie

"Hello." The unfamiliar male voice hesitates when I answer the phone. "Is this Mrs. Weatherill?"

A chill goes up my spine. I sit down and cautiously respond, "Yes?"

A loudspeaker in the background announces a flight and drowns out his response.

"I'm sorry, I didn't get that," I say.

"Hi, uh, you don't know me, but I promised I would call you when I got back. I'm Antonio Alesti. Your husband and I were roommates."

"Wow, thanks for calling. Where are you?"

"Seattle Airport, between flights."

"Welcome back. I'm so glad you called." It's a relief to talk to someone who actually made it back.

"Yeah, it's great to be here." I hear a smile in his voice. "I think he was a good roommate," he continues, searching for something more to say.

"I think he is, too." I can't resist teasing this fellow Jim portrayed as such a smooth ladies' man.

Alesti coughs as if he inhaled instead of swallowing. "Umm, you guys are more, uh, intimate, if you know what I mean. We just talked a lot."

"We talk a lot, too," I say.

A loudspeaker announces another flight.

He clears his throat. "Well, I gotta go."

"Thanks again. I'll let Jim know you called. Have a good trip." Apparently, Jim hadn't warned him about me.

Vietnam

I've got a new guy, Mister Gordon, flying with me. I've been in country too long to ask him about the States, and he hasn't been here long enough to talk about the war. But, we talk.

"People back in the States are against the war," he says.

"Nobody likes war."

"Lots of protests." Gordon shakes his head.

"I guess I'll get to see for myself pretty soon."

"It's not the same place you left."

I think it's a joke and laugh a little to myself. "America has always cared about her soldiers."

"We're cogs in a political wheel. Trust me, soldiers are pariahs; they're cursed."

I feel a little unsettled. I would never have talked this way as a newcomer. The old pilots would have reached across the cockpit and slapped me silly.

"We're the fuel that turns the wheel. When we get back to the States they'll use the wheel to crush us," Gordon concludes.

I don't have time for what he's talking about. We're in flight above Vietnam, and I'm thinking Vietnam. It's how you stay alive here. Sure, we've seen the front change during the war. We've taken ridges and given them back. I don't like it; in fact it revolts me, but I can't quit. I promised my country.

I daydream, even though I shouldn't. It's a short daydream because I know better. I don't expect much. I try hard to keep my dreams off the battlefield. They're difficult enough in my sleep. I get off a plane at an airport. There's music and banners and waving and yelling and soldiers streaming off the plane behind me.

We're carried away on the shoulders of the crowd, and I am home.

"Mister Gordon, do you know where you are?" I ask.

"What do you mean?"

"Where the hell are you? Look out your window. You see America out there?"

"No," he says.

"You think the NVA give a shit about protesters and wheels and cogs?"

"They should, and so should you."

"All I care about is staying alive," I respond. "All they care about is shooting down American helicopters and killing their crews. You need to take a moment and think about this basic NVA goal."

We land at Ban Me Thout East to get our first load along with the daily logistics pad briefing. The log pad launches helicopters as fast as it can load them.

A couple C-123 spray planes dressed up like crop dusters taxi toward the steel-planked runway. The east side of the airfield holds a rising mountain of discarded 55-gallon drums emptied by the aerial spraying. The Montagnards who live in the highlands around the city cart the drums off and use them for any number of things in their villages.

Over a period of days, I watch a young boy pound away with a chisel and rock to cut the top off a drum. A week later, he carries the drum out to a grass meadow, about a kilometer from the airfield. The barrel sits below the point in the sky where pilots call the tower at Ban Me Thout East Airfield for landing instructions. It's the meadow where the family elephant grazes.

The boy carries water, bucket by bucket, up a steep ravine. He has the barrel full of creek water, as we arrive to land at Ban Me Thout. I slow the helicopter to view the scene. The elephant lumbers up to the small boy and curls his huge trunk around the child, lifting him off the ground. The smile on my face is the widest it's been in weeks.

The elephant puts the child down and pushes its trunk deep into the drum of water. Suddenly, it steps back rigidly, staggers, and falls over on its side.

Two hours later we are in the same place in the sky, returning from another mission. The elephant is on its side, its legs straight out. At least ten people circle the body. Someone dressed in embroidered robes swings an incense burner. The child who worked so hard on the barrel is in the tall grass twenty meters away, prostrate on the ground.

I close my eyes and tears squeeze out.

What the hell is in those barrels?

*   *   *

I get a break from flying with another faceless new guy. Travis and I are assigned together for today's missions. What a treat it is to fly with someone who knows what's going on. We've just fueled and parked at the side of the log pad. It's time for lunch.

Two captains wearing Army Chemical Corps insignias come aboard and enter the companionway of our Chinook. "We need you," one says.

I get on the radio with the logistics pad. Because Travis has been in country longer than I have, we use his call sign. "Log Control, Windy Four Seven."

"Go ahead, Windy."

"Listen, we've got two chemical captains here. They tell us we're supposed to go with them. What gives? I thought we were all yours today."

"I don't know. Stand by."

"Standing by."

Log Control makes a few calls. It takes long enough for us to finish our C-ration fare.

"Windy Four Seven, Log Control."

"Go ahead, Sir," I reply.

"They didn't tell me what it's about, but the thing has the general's seal of approval."

"Great," I say under my breath. "Thank you, Control," I answer. "This means we've got to make up the ammo sorties," I whine to Travis. "Who else is around to carry the stuff?"

"Who really cares?" Travis yawns. "You, maybe; me, maybe; Steele and Jacaby and Wellish; who the hell else needs to care?"

"Hey, Mister Travis," Jacaby calls, "Put me down for not caring, Sir."

"Yeah, yeah," I mutter. Travis is right.

"Look at it as another new adventure," Travis offers.

As we talk, six men come aboard to modify the interior of the Chinook. They install rollers similar to those warehouse men use to slide cases of vegetables and canned goods out of freight trucks back home. Then, parallel lines of twelve 55-gallon drums are loaded on the two roller tracks. The chemical men secure both rows of barrels.

Each drum is labeled with diamond-shaped chemical symbols and wrapped in detonation cord with an eleven-second fuse. The fuses are connected to lengths of braided stainless steel wire. We pull our winch line through a series of rollers. This stretches the cable along the top of the Chinook like a clothesline. The fuse lanyards are then hooked onto the winch line with metal clips.

We are now a bomber. *Are these barrels carrying the same stuff the elephant drank,* I wonder.

"Hey, Mister Travis," Steele says, standing in the Chinook's companionway.

Travis looks back. "Huh?"

"A couple presents for the pilots." He hands us each a gas mask and then goes aft.

A chemical captain comes up next. "One of you has to wear his mask at all times," he orders.

"Starting when?" Travis asks.

"Starting now."

Travis takes out his Zippo with his name engraved on one side. "Name or blank?"

"Blank."

Travis flips. I win.

What a sight Travis becomes. He's strapped in his seat in his red-clay stained, sweat-fanned fatigues. Strapped to his left thigh is his survival pack. Taped to his right thigh are four extra clips for his .45-caliber pistol, which is strapped under his left armpit. Hanging from his shoulders, covering his chest, is his body armor. The chest plate has a pocket in the middle front, stuffed with a pack of cigarettes, two cigars, his Zippo, the plastic spoon he eats his C-rations with, and a little book of today's communication frequencies.

At his feet, in the helicopter chin bubble, is his flak jacket. On his head is his ballistic helmet with a wire off the side to plug him into the war, and his face is covered with a gas mask. He looks like something out of Buck Rogers.

We are about to play a piece in an elaborate plan. The plains west of Ban Me Thout teem with NVA. Ban Me Thout is a prized goal of the NVA. Since they have not been able to take Duc Lap, they will simply go around it; next stop, our temporary home.

The invading army needs to cross the Ea Krong River at predictable fording points. Our job is to block the river banks at those places. We takeoff into a developing afternoon squall line. Halfway along our flight to the infiltration routes, the chemical men begin preparations.

We arrive at the river and follow it to our first point. We level our Chinook at the prescribed altitude at the direction of the chemists, and the chemical crew pushes the barrels out the back. The cans fall into space, pull free of the fuse lanyard, drop into the jungle canopy and explode. We make three runs at each location, saturating the area from the ground to the top of the jungle canopy.

When we load for our seventh run out, working the third fording point, I ask a dumb question to one of the chemical captains. "How long does this stuff last?"

"Oh, only about two weeks. Effectively, that is."

"That long, huh," I state naïvely, watching Travis strap on his mask. Travis and I shrug an "okay, I guess" at one another.

"Effectively," the chemical captain repeats.

"What's that mean?"

"The normal human will suffocate within, oh, eight to ten minutes. It takes about two to three minutes for them to realize they're in it, and by then it's too late, even if they mask up."

"Are you serious?" We're spreading enough for a twenty-minute hike. My stomach constricts.

Travis looks at me, his eyes bulging behind the gas mask lenses.

"Yeah, pretty neat, huh," the captain says, smiling.

Mission seven. With this load we will have dropped 168 cans of this stuff. Where is reality? It's right in front of us. We're suffocating in it, 55 gallons at a time.

Travis, Jacaby, Wellish, Steele, and I mask up and start the bird. Afternoon thunderstorms are fully grown now. The sun is there, somewhere behind the pitch black thunderstorm bottoms, and walls of rain. We go in and out of the cloud bases, trying to hide our trail and our destination and ourselves.

"We're unstrapping the cans," Steele informs.

Our helicopter emerges from the side of a cloud, and we face a rain so dark we can't see the ground. A cloud rolls over us and tosses us with turbulence.

A chemical captain comes up to the cockpit. "Take her down to eleven hundred feet." He grabs the companionway strap. "And try to keep it steady."

The helicopter drops into an air pocket.

"You do your job and I'll do mine." The mask muffles Travis' voice.

"What?"

I point to the altimeter and make a level sign with my hand. Chemical man gives me an okay, points to his watch and holds up two fingers. The helicopter lurches and bangs him against the companionway wall.

I punch the sweep second button on my clock. "Get ready, Steele, two minutes."

"What the hell is that?" Travis says through his mask into his boom mike.

A rolling cloud forms directly in front of us. When we enter it, our airspeed falls off and we are held in place. Then, the helicopter pitches up violently, yaws sideways, and rolls uncontrollably. A drum on the starboard rack, the drum directly behind Travis, the drum slated to be the last out, crashes against the right side of the helicopter. It hits Jacaby in the hip and pins his right knee against the Chinook's aluminum side. The fuse pin pulls out. Eleven seconds to detonation.

"Live fuse!" Jacaby yelps in pain.

"Get these barrels out of here!" Steele screams.

Everybody in the back of the Chinook leans into the drums in controlled panic. Travis holds the nose up and pulls every ounce of power the engines can give.

The last drum leaves our desperate helicopter at eternity second ten.

Then eleven.

The explosion pitches the Chinook on its nose. On our instrument panel all the red warning lights flash on for a split second, then a white cloud floods the helicopter. Everything disappears. I can't catch my breath. Vapor fills the inside of my gas mask.

I wipe the white film off the lenses of my mask, but I can't wipe the fog off the inside. I reach over and open the window. The murky jungle canopy comes into view at a strange angle. I move the cyclic stick around until the jungle canopy levels, and push the rudder pedals until the wind blows the rain through the window onto my mask. I let it rain in the cockpit.

"Travis!" I call out.

"What?" He's wiping the lenses of his mask.

"I'm rinsing my mask off," I tell him.

"Yeah, I'm with you. I see what you're doing."

"You look like a snowman," I say.

"It's irrelevant. We may be fucked," he says, dusting the powder off his flight instruments. "Okay, I've got an attitude indicator, now. Damn, it's hard to breathe."

I stick my head out the cockpit window, and the driving rain beats against my mask. Water runs down my neck. I pull off the mask, suck a lung full of sweet Central Highlands squall line air into my body, and cram my face back into my wet mask. "Your turn."

Travis takes control again, opens his window, and pushes the rudder pedals to spray himself with water.

"Steele? What's it look like back there?" Travis asks.

"Well, number two engine is hanging by one engine mount. Part of the ramp's gone, and a whole bunch of aluminum ain't here anymore. Plus lot of noises I've never heard."

"Wellish?"

"Here."

"Jacaby?"

"I'm with him," Wellish answers. "His knee's all screwed up."

"As if I didn't know, asshole," Jacaby swears into the ship's intercom.

"Hey, we've got to get back. A couple of these chemical guys are messed up bad," Steele calls. "And some of the chemical guys went out the back from the explosion. They didn't have time to hook up."

"We can't help them; we may just be able to help ourselves," Travis says.

The helicopter shakes like a freight train is rushing by and there's a loud bang; the Chinook yaws and sags in the sky.

Wellish looks out the right gun port. "Sir, the right engine just fell off."

I work the emergency check list, and Travis turns us back toward Ban Me Thout. I relay our position in map coordinates and our problem to a gun team about halfway between us and Ban Me Thout. The gun team turns around to come to our aid.

"Windy Four Seven, High Station." It's the Air Force controller working fighter jets along the border to our west.

"High Station, Windy Four Seven, go ahead," I answer.

"We have your coordinates. We will cover you."

"Thank you, High Station."

The number one engine overheats and the oil pressure bounces off zero. It holds together long enough to get us to a small village about eighteen kilometers south of Ban Me Thout City. The front of the number one engine blows off as we roll to a stop in the dirt.

The Huey gun team orbits above us; a Dustoff hovers alongside the cockpit.

"We've got some folks for you, Dustoff," I call over.

"Everybody's got folks for us. Your bird looks pretty beat up, Windy."

We help Steele load the injured chemical guys, and we carry Jacaby to a second Dustoff that has just landed. Then, we sit in the grass beside our mortally wounded helicopter, dust ourselves off, and survey the damage. My smokes are ruined from the cockpit rain, and I throw the soggy pack on the ground. Steele pulls out two cigarettes and lights them. When he hands me a cigarette, his eyes glisten.

The storm that held our fate catches up with us and drenches us again. I can't tell rain from tears; it's good timing. A slick shows up, and the rest of us climb on and ride back to Ban Me Thout.

Riverside, California: Annie

Maryanne is in her playpen, alternating between trying to crawl and wrestling with her teddy bear that's as big as she is. The whole time, she babbles a commentary on her activities. I think about taking her outside and how much fun it is to watch her discover the world.

Because of her, I begin to notice beauty again in small things, such as the lace that tree shadows make on the driveway, how grass waves and clouds drift. I guess we see the same sky Jim flies in, only a different part of it.

Now that Jim's time is short, every day is a week long. My stomach burns and I'm too restless to sit still. I can almost dare to dream we are together again in each other's arms in our own home where we run things our way, do things with our own friends, and make plans for our little family.

PART 13
NOVEMBER 1968
20 DAYS TO GO

Final Days

Vietnam

We shake hands and hug each other beside the runway of
Ban Me Thout East Airfield before Travis leaves on a
Herc for Phu Hiep. His time is up. It's his turn to take the
Big Bird home. No one else can leave the war. Travis
leaves alone.

A few days later, the flight surgeon sends Overton
and me to Phu Hiep for a two-day rest. A $10 bill lies on
my bed beside a note:

> Weatherill, I have a strange combination of
> memory and expectation in my head. I'm traveling
> as light as possible. It'll take all my strength to
> carry my heart. Alesti told me to get you a kite,
> but Duc Lap was sold out. Sorry. See you on the
> other side, Travis.

I'm happy and grateful for my friends who are out of
this war: Captain Dodge, Lieutenant Kase, Misters
Peters, Miller and Styki. However, the loss of my
confidants, Alesti and Travis, is almost a mortal wound. I
lie on my bunk and sleep for twenty-two hours. While I
sleep, we get four new pilots.

I wake up, clean up, and walk to the flight surgeon's
office for a chat and look-see. He says, "Get some chow
and get back to work. Don't forget your malaria pills."

I walk to the mess hall, talk the cook out of two cold
sandwiches and take them to our bar. Overton is behind

the counter, putting fresh ice in his glass and pouring his favorite bourbon.

"What's your pleasure?" He asks.

"Scotch, please." I take out my smokes and light up. "Been here long?"

"Sleep is over rated." He passes me a drink.

"Sandwich?" I offer.

"Thanks. Seen any of the new guys yet?" Overton asks.

"Nope."

"Well, I have. Seem okay, except one."

"How so?"

"Two came back for a second tour to be lieutenants and fly Chinooks," he says.

"And the others?"

"One seems normal. The other is some sort of reservist who claims he didn't know what he was signing. He's complaining to the C.O."

"The C.O.'s back?"

"Yep, he came to help you get the new guys ready."

"Anything else?" I ask.

"Isaac's ship got hit. Lost both his gunners to the hospital tent in Ban Me Thout. And listen to this: Isaac put his left hand in the way of a bullet. I guess they looked all over the cockpit for his finger so they could try to sew it back on. No one said they found it, though."

"Holy cow."

"I'm not sure where he is right now. I think maybe Japan." Overton shakes his head. "It's good he draws with his right hand."

I take a bite of my sandwich and wash it down with scotch.

"And something else."

"What?"

"Morrow." Overton pauses. "Major Black got the list of grievances that Lieutenant Kase put together before he left. The stuff got lost and then found."

"Sure it did," I mutter. "What's the major going to do?"

"It's what he did. He told Morrow he should be tried for savagery. Morrow took a transfer out of here."

"Just somebody else's problem," I say.

"I'm not sure I understand you."

"Me neither."

I leave the bar and walk to our post office to pick up my mail. Just feeling the letters is like holding a chair for my wife at the table or passing the vegetables at dinner. My arms ache to hold our daughter. My eyes burn to see her.

In the stack is a letter from Father Thomas. I open it first. His handwriting is almost as bad as mine:

> Mister Weatherill, I pray this finds you well. I cannot tell you where I am. But, you were right. I don't regret what I did, and please don't feel any remorse. I can tell you the time at the firebase opened my eyes wider than I could ever have imagined. Life and death so incredibly close together. I enjoyed our friendship and talks and I will miss them, Father Thomas.

I pull the envelope away from the letter. There is no postmark, no return address, only my address, only my name. Damn them.

-37-

Ambush

Vietnam

We haul sling loads of fuel blivets to firebase Kingpin, southwest of Duc Lap. The area around Duc Lap looks like an occupied war memorial disguised as the surface of the moon.

Mister Gordon sits next to me. He's been here five weeks now, and his monologues on the intercom about the war, politicians, and his wife are a constant disruption.

"Windy Seven Zero, Kingpin," the firebase calls.

"Windy Seven Zero," I take the call.

"ETA?"

"Five minutes," I estimate.

"Scrambler on?"

"Affirmative, we're discrete."

"Fuel state?"

"Just above half-full." We expect to land, then bring some grunts back to Ban Me Thout and end our day.

"We've got a change of mission," the firebase informs.

"Go ahead," I respond.

"We have a Huey down on Highway 14. There's a recovery team in now. We need you to extract the ship."

"You can see the NVA doing their morning exercises over there. You want us to land on their street? If the people are out, what's the beef?"

"We got a couple NVA brass on a raid last night. Some stuff got left behind. We want the Huey."

"Okay. Give us the coordinates," I say.

"I'll get back, Windy."

"And, Kingpin, Windy is on final."

"Why didn't they take the damn papers with them?" Steele asks.

"Maybe they were running for their lives," I suggest.

We approach the firebase to deliver the blivets. Steele, on the floor, his head hanging through the hook well, gives me hover directions. "Not bad for an old fart," he says as the bladders of fuel release behind two armored personnel carriers.

"I wish I had a camera," Jacaby adds. Not wanting to be called a loafer, he flies with a knee brace.

Kingpin breaks in. A seven-man recovery team is at the wrecked Huey and will have it ready to go. When the extraction is over, the Huey that put the team on the road will come back and get them. So, come and get it, simple.

Air cover will be there: two Loaches, light observation helicopters, equipped with a pilot-operated machine gun mounted to the left side of the aircraft, and a right door gunner with his own machine gun; four Huey gunships, each with a Gatling gun, rocket pods, and two door gunners. On High Station, two F-100 fighters will provide cover with 20 mm cannons and napalm. Simple. Uh huh.

Rather than take on fuel, we hover over Kingpin, burning off a little extra weight. The other aircraft on the mission fly toward the firebase. Our armada joined, we fly to Highway 14, which runs near the Cambodia-Vietnam border. The Loaches and the Hueys go into their tactical orbits. We hover above the jungle canopy at a hole large enough for the wreck to pass through and then let our hoist line completely out.

"They're dragging the line away from the hole, Sir," Steele says from his vantage point.

"Fifty more feet, Windy," the recovery leader requests.

"That's it, buddy. We're all out," I answer, with our blades inches above the trees. "We can't reach from here."

"Hey, Windy, Loach One," a voice breaks in.

"Windy."

"You can get below the canopy over here. We can get on the highway," Loach One suggests.

I look south. The Loach pilot descends below the top layer of jungle about 300 feet away. "Can we fit?"

"I think so. Come on."

We come up.

"We're out of the trees. The line will be all in, in just a minute," Steele says, as he and Wellish pull up our cable, coiling it carefully on the Chinook's floor.

"Line's in," Steele advises.

I hover to the other canopy hole.

"You got the idea, Recovery?" I ask.

"Yeah, we're running thirty-five feet of sling toward the hole. Loach One is right above us."

We carefully descend through the opening and land on the road. Then, we move toward the wrecked Huey, where two recovery team members stand at the end of the sling line. As we roll along the road, the second Loach descends behind us, guarding our rear.

"Loach Two is on the road."

One recovery man bends against the winds of our Chinook's rotor system as he runs toward us and disappears under the belly.

"Line's going out," Steele calls.

The recovery man reappears under our chin bubbles and drags our cable toward the end of the sling. As the cable weight increases, a second man runs to help. Five other recovery team members circle the sling end. Finally, the cable and the sling are connected.

"Start pulling, Windy!" the recovery leader yells.

"You want to get on with us, Recovery," I ask, "long as we're here?"

"We'll make sure you get out okay. We'll take the Huey ride out. Thanks for the offer."

The moment I pull the line taunt, the dead Huey rolls on its side and life changes. Dozens of bullets cut down the seven recovery men where they stand.

"Jesus, it's an ambush!" Loach One yells on the air-net. "Let's get out! Let's get out!"

"Blow the line, Steele! Gordon, cover the controls; let's not run into anything!" I look over to make sure Gordon is on the controls and the important radio switch at his finger tip.

Steele punches the button on the side of the .45-caliber guillotine to sever the braided cable. It doesn't fire. "No cut! God, it doesn't work! No cut! No cut! These fucking things; I'll kill the sons-a-bitches!"

The door gunners open fire at people hanging in trees. The sound of bullets entering our aluminum home is sickening.

"Gordon we're stuck to the load. Call High Station. Have their jets napalm both sides of the road," I order.

Meanwhile, gunships rain thousands of rounds into the trees. Bodies fall like leaves blown by winter's wind. The Loach pilots pedal turn to protect our engines and our cockpit. The door gunner in Loach One, directly ahead of our cockpit, is hit. His gun stops firing and he hangs in his harness. Smoke pours from the Loach engine.

We drag the Huey along the highway toward the canopy hole. My left hand has a death grip on the thrust lever, ensuring maximum power when we need it. I control the cyclic with my right hand and follow the door gunners' directions as they lead us back to the opening in the canopy. I want to fire my automatic rifle out my window, but I don't have enough hands. I hope this is a nightmare.

I don't hear Gordon's call to High Station. He's slumped in his seat.

"Steele, Gordon's gone. Get up here, please!"

"Yes, Sir!"

I squeeze the radio switch on my cyclic stick. "High Station, High Station, send your jets; napalm, napalm both sides. Help us!"

Someone screams behind me. I look back. Jacaby rolls on his back on the floor. Blood trickles down his face.

Into all this Gordon looks at me. "I'll lose my wife!" he exclaims.

Steele puts a compress against Jacaby's head and. Jacaby moans. It's a good sound: it means he's still alive.

I yell at Gordon. "Wake up! God dammit, we need your help!"

He stares at me hollow-eyed. "She can't have the children."

Steele's with us in the cockpit now. We're at the opening in the leafy canopy. We begin our ascent through the trees.

"High Station jets will deliver in one minute. Get those gunships out of the way," comes over our radio.

"We're moving," a gunship reports. "The Chinook and the Loaches are still on the highway."

"High Station understands."

The number one engine decelerates. "Gordon, hit the emergency trim! Stop the spool down!" I order.

Gordon just sits. "Tell them to stop shooting!" he sobs.

"Steele, the trim!" I yell.

"Kingpin, Gun Two, over," the gunship breaks in.

"Kingpin."

"All hell's broke loose over here. Alert Dustoff." The pilot rolls his gunship around to cover the jets.

Steele reaches the trim switch on the center console and pushes the trim override, manually feeding fuel into the engine. It spools back up sluggishly. "Not good, Boss."

"No shit!"

"You got this nuthouse to yourself, Sir. I'm getting on Jacaby's gun."

"Thanks, Steele."

The trees around us explode in brilliant yellow orange. The fighters have arrived. I envy their speed.

"High Lead is coming around for a strafing run."

"Two is coming around."

"How's the engine?" Steele asks me.

"It's stuck at full power now. We'll take it!" I answer. We're coming out of the jungle.

"Windy, Loach one, I have to go now."

"I owe you," I say.

"Windy, Loach Two. You've got a problem. They're climbing on the load!"

Sure as hell they are. We've started up with the load weight, and it's gotten heavier, stopping our rise. "Can you shoot 'em off?" I ask.

"If I have enough ammo left. We're working on it."

"Windy Seven Zero, High Lead, we need you out of there," the jet pilot breaks in.

"Impossible at the moment, we're stuck here."

"High Lead will delay."

"Two copies," High Lead's wingman says.

"We've got you, Windy," Gun One says, flying straight at us. The Huey adds rockets and bullets to the flames.

Steele and Wellish fire straight down.

We begin to lift. We're almost free. Up. Up. Slowly up.

"We're free!" Steele and Wellish shout, still firing their weapons.

"Tell me Loach Two is out," I say.

"He's coming out now! He's clear!" Wellish reports.

"Kingpin, Windy Seven Zero needs Dustoff," I call.

"Just get here, Windy," firebase Kingpin answers.

In minutes we're at Kingpin. The dangling Huey smashes into the ground inside the camp's trip wires. We hover down to get our cable hook released and reel the line in. Then, we hover to the refueling pad for medical help and JP-4. The fighter jets race over Kingpin and across our Chinook to strafe the road again.

My shaking hands fight to light a cigarette. I blow the smoke out the left cockpit window and watch a rocket trail come out of the jungle, just missing one of the jets. I swallow a mouthful of smoke.

Fuel hoses replenish our tanks while medics carry Jacaby off our ship to a waiting Dustoff. The number one engine continues to run at full throttle.

We lift off and fly for Ban Me Thout. I can't stop shaking.

Gordon's body slumps against the right side of his seat. He's gone somewhere in his mind. I'd like to kill him.

I call ahead to operations about Gordon. When we land, medics lead Gordon away. I close the fuel valve to the number one engine with the fire handle and try to light another cigarette with my shaking hands.

Home

Vietnam

After a couple more days, the C.O. sends me back to Phu
Hiep and the coast. I fly log missions, supplying the
Koreans for a week, and then it's over for me. Eight other
pilots are back in Phu Hiep to trade broken helicopters for
repaired ones. The aircraft commanders, I know. Some
have become friends. Most of the co-pilots are not
familiar.

Overton answers my knock on his hooch door.
"Congratulations, you're headed home. Come in! Come
in!"

"I want to thank you for all your help at Mile High.
Your calls got us into the clearing. I don't remember
thanking you properly," I say.

"We shook hands on the heliport. That was enough."

"When we were in the tree roots you said you wanted
an M2, so I brought you mine. I hope it serves you well." I
hand him the gun.

On my way to the bar, I pass Lieutenant Drum. He
ignores my eye contact and says nothing as we pass. It's
probably best.

Before he went stateside, Isaac painted a picture of
me with my head out the cockpit window. The payload
slung under the helicopter is a pizza. It's added to the
others hanging on the bar walls. I have a few drinks with
Overton and tonight slips into tomorrow.

The sound of the morning launch wakes me at 5 a.m. I will leave for the airport at 3 p.m. I sit in my room, remembering my friends. Finally, I take down my posters of Humphrey Bogart and Bob Dylan and walk them across to Lock and Load's barber shop. I help him put them on his shop's walls. My last haircut is free.

I take the broken Falcon kite off the ceiling above my bed and carry it gingerly to our bar. The C.O. gave me permission to mount it on the wall as a permanent part of company history.

Back in my room I pack my calendar, letters from home, the bulk of my photographs, and a chess set I had Alesti buy in Hong Kong as a present for my brother. On top of the pile, I put the fuse lanyard from the 55-gallon drum that smashed Jacaby's knee.

Memories wander in my mind, and I feel I'm packing for a dead man. Most of me is ready to leave, but some of me isn't. I sit on my cot and smoke a cigarette. I'm alone and afraid to leave my hooch; afraid that when I leave it I'll never get it back; I'm abandoning my youth. I splash cold water from our sink on my face and hear laughter and sorrow in my head. It's hard to leave yourself behind.

Without my posters, Alesti's voice, Travis' smile, the plywood walls turn unfamiliar, unfriendly. I feel as hollow as the day I arrived in country. My unknown fate that I brought to the war, I now will carry home.

Finally, time to go. I have two foot lockers and my duffel. I open my hooch door, looking for some local workers to help me carry my baggage. No men are in sight. The maids are gone, too.

"Wouldn't you know it," I mutter, going back in my room to start the task alone. After a moment there's a knock on the door.

"Yes. Come in!"

It's our interpreter, Mister Phong. "Sir, please come with me."

"What's up, Mister Phong?"

"Sir, please."

I walk out the door and see three workers. As I leave the room, they enter and carry my items out behind me. I hear murmurs and rustling of people approaching.

Lock and Load, swinging an incense burner on a chain, comes around the end of the hooches. Four hooch maids follow with a group of children. The women carry colorful banners.

"Why?"

"They will miss you, Mister Weatherill. Please believe."

"Thank you, Mister Phong." I'm shocked. I don't know what to say. It's amazing what a playground will do.

I leave Vietnam with 1,341 combat hours in my log book.

Cam Ranh Bay, Vietnam

> *Cam Ranh Bay*
> *Waiting for the plane out,*
> *A World Airways plane.*
> *We are quarantined;*
> *We have Homebound,*
> *A rare disease.*

Over the Pacific Ocean

After five hours, we stop in Japan for fuel for the jet. After flying twelve more hours, we land at Seattle International Airport. America after a year. America! Everyone wants off the plane and onto America. Total strangers seventeen hours ago, we now shake hands and slap one another on the back. We pass immigrations and clear customs. We leave our holding area. We're back.

A crowd waits outside customs. Many have welcome signs and scream in glee when they see their loved one, and there is happy mayhem. Those of us who do not end our journey here at Seattle continue walking. We meet a second group. They, too, carry banners. This group is rowdy, and Port of Seattle Police officers are conspicuous. The signs here say "Baby Killers," "Government Filth," "Stop the War." I'm spit on. And I'm spit on again.

A police officer pushes through. He looks me in the eyes. "I'm sorry, son."

"Can I borrow your pistol?" I ask.

He doesn't answer.

We're escorted to a private area and hidden in the Seattle Airport complex. We're shown to showers, and clean ourselves of the seventeen-hour plane ride. It's impossible to wipe off the spit or the shock. I change into a clean uniform from my duffel bag.

After five hours, I get on a Western Airlines jet for the ride to Los Angeles and the reunion with my family. I'm heading to my first sight of our daughter, now almost eight months old.

In the air south of Seattle a stewardesses comes to my seat. "Are you getting off in San Francisco?"

"No."

"Then you're not on your way to Vietnam?"

"No. I just returned."

"You're going home?"

"Yes. Los Angeles. Him, too." I point to another American I met while waiting in the Seattle Airport.

"Congratulations! Scotch, huh?" she says looking at the miniature on my tray table.

"Yes, please."

She disappears toward the front of the airplane. After a few minutes she returns with a handful of small scotch bottles and another meal. My compatriot, a few seats ahead, is treated similarly. He leans around in his seat and makes an okay sign with his fingers.

I give him a thumbs up.

The aircraft P.A. crackles to life above the seats.

"Ladies and Gentlemen, this is your captain speaking. It is with great honor and deep appreciation that I, along with this flight crew and Western Airlines, welcome two of our passengers back home from Vietnam. We want to thank them for their sacrifice and their service."

People look around from their seats. After a moment the plane erupts in applause. Some people even get out of their seats and come by to shake our hands.

We're in and out of San Francisco in less than an hour. Finally, L.A., we are here. Home, close enough.

Riverside, California: Annie

We pile into the Oldsmobile with Fred and Marie in front and Janie, Maryanne and me in back. Our destination is the Los Angeles International Airport. Our one-year countdown has shrunk to hours, now. Here we come, L.A.

We chat about the homecoming celebration planned for the weekend, and other lighthearted topics. For me, however, the mood is cautious exhilaration, as if carefree joy is a new outfit that doesn't quite fit. It's hard to wriggle out of the anxiety I've worn so long that it feels like my skin. I'm afraid to be so happy; afraid to believe this is real.

Maryanne's smile tugs at my thoughts and I'm filled with gratitude for this beautiful, healthy child. I'm thankful for God's loan of the guardian angel who took on the challenge to protect Jim and bring him safely home.

At the airport, we find our way to the gate. Another eager group gathers nearby. Now, the countdown is in minutes. Through the window, we watch the plane pull up to the gate. Time is suspended as we wait. Eventually, passengers in slow motion straggle off the plane.

We glimpse a military uniform among the passengers in the jetway. The soldier appears, and the group next to us erupts in cheers and tears and mobs the man.

Then, Jim appears and it's our turn.

In his arms, I've come home, too.

Postscript

In the Officers' Club at Fort Benning, Georgia, I crossed trails with the gunship pilots who saved our lives in Laos. It was pure luck and proof of this small world. We shook hands, drank whiskey, hugged, and went our separate ways.

Travis couldn't find himself in America after he got back. His American vision eluded him and his pride was in his uniform and his service. He accepted a promotion to captain and returned to Vietnam. He died as a result of hostile fire. I will see you on the other side, Travis, I promise.

I found out what was in the barrel that killed the elephant.

* * *

In my mind are places dust will never fall and

In my heart old friends laugh and toast life;

To the pulse beat that is the difference between us.

Epilogue

This memoir ends more than four decades of silence on my part. We who were there honor daily the sacrifice of those who died in service to America. The abuse and distortions heaped upon their legacy is a filthy blot on America's soul. We survivors know how easy it is to hurt; how the pendulum swing is meaningless if there is no substance in its arc.

God bless America.

Glossary

ADF: Automatic Direction Finder to get a bearing to or from a transmitter, usually located near an airport. The ADF receiver also contained AM radio frequencies.

AFT: Rearward. Moving from front to back is moving aft.

Anti-war Protesters: Demonstrated in opposition to the draft and the war. Some served time in jail.

APC: Armored Personnel Carrier transported soldiers, patrolled highways, and supported convoys.

Arc Light: B-52 bombing missions on infiltration routes and enemy massing.

Armored Seat: Helicopter pilot seats had armor on the window side, seat bottom, and seat back.

Blivet: Rubber barrel used to transport fuel, etc.

Blood Chit: Cloth with the U.S. flag image above multilingual requests for assistance and offering a reward for help getting the bearer back to safety.

Bunker: A fortified hole normally shored with wood or pierced steel planks and lined with sandbags. At the bottom of the entry stairs was a trench backed by a high wood wall. Grenades thrown in the bunker were supposed to bounce off this wall, deflect into the trench, and explode without harming the soldiers in the bunker.

Camp Holloway: A U.S. Army helicopter base just south of Pleiku City and named after Warrant Officer Charles E. Holloway who was killed in action in December 1962.

Chest Plate or Chicken Plate: Pilots wore heavy ceramic body armor to cover the chest and abdomen while flying.

Citations: Descriptions of valor.

Civvies: Non-military clothing worn when out of uniform.

Collective Stick: Control stick attached to the helicopter floor at the pilots' left side used to make the helicopter go up or down. Called thrust lever in Chinooks.

Concertina or Razor Wire: Coiled wire with blades formed into the wire and strung in loops as a defensive boundary.

Conex: Slang term for the metal box holding radios and targeting computers used to aim firebase cannon. The conex is approximately 8' x 8' x 8'.

Conscientious Objector: Someone who opposed the war for religious or personal reasons. Some volunteered to serve in combat, often as a radio operator or medic.

C-Ration: Combat meals, such as ham and lima beans, jam, cookies, pound cake, or crackers, packaged in cans.

Cyclic Stick: Stands up from the floor of the helicopter between the pilot's legs and controls the helicopter's movement along longitudinal and lateral axes.

Cypher: Scrambles radio transmissions to make them untranslatable to the enemy.

Dead Reckoning: Time, distance, heading and speed are used to navigate. It's also known as pencil and paper navigation.

Deros: Date eligible to return from overseas; the day a soldier was scheduled to go home.

Dial "O" for Operator: Yesterday's 9-1-1. Before 9-1-1 emergency centers, people dialed "O" (zero) to get the operator to connect to emergency services.

Discrete: Radio transmissions scrambled through a cypher.

DMZ: Demilitarized zone divided North and South Vietnam.

Donut Dollies: Female Red Cross volunteers, nicknamed by soldiers in the Korean War because the Red Cross had donut-making machines.

Draft Dodger: Someone eligible to serve but avoided the draft and military service, sometimes leaving the U.S.A. Later, Presidents Ford and Carter pardoned these people, some of whom later rose to high station in the U.S. government.

Dustoff: Call sign of medical evacuation aircraft, on call 24/7, normally flown with UH-1 Huey helicopters.

ETA: Estimated time of arrival.

Evacuation Hospital: Evac, a war zone military hospital.

FAC: Forward Air Controllers identified targets for fighters flying ground support sorties.

Firebase: An artillery base, some accessible only by helicopter. Cannon fire provided support to soldiers within range of their guns.

Fleshette: Small steel darts fired by cannon during overrun situations, normally at point blank range. Each cannon round contained approximately 1,500 darts.

FM Homing: FM radios used by infantry units for communication also allowed aircraft to home in on the radio position.

Ground Resonance: Shock absorbers and tires, parts of the helicopter's landing gear, are capable of bouncing against themselves. The result is an intense vibration that can increase rapidly and will destroy the helicopter if not stopped.

Grunt: Affectionate nickname for U.S. infantry soldiers; hardworking, honorable, and heroic Americans asked to do the impossible.

Gunship: UH-1 Huey helicopter fitted with Gatling guns and rocket pods; crewed by two pilots and two door gunners to create an armed airborne support platform. Huey gunships normally flew in flights of two aircraft.

Herc: The C-130 Hercules, a four engine cargo aircraft.

High Station: Aircraft controllers, orbiting the battlefield at high altitude, managed the resources of fighter jets for ground support.

Ho Chi Minh Trail: The route used by infiltrating NVA soldiers. It primarily followed the borders of Laos and Cambodia with Vietnam. Its location made it difficult to stem the flow of men and materiel. The triple canopy jungle aided in hiding the NVA forces.

Hooch: Living quarters ranging from bunkers to tents to wooden structures.

Howitzer Casing: The shell of the howitzer round.

Huey: The Bell UH-1 helicopter, crewed by two pilots and two gunners, carried ammo, fuel, people, food; and performed combat insertions and medical evacuations.

Ident: The aviation request to electronically identify an aircraft by activating its transponder which showed up on radar and located the aircraft.

IP: An instructor pilot flew with new pilots to ensure they knew the workings of the aircraft before being released into combat.

Kilometer: 0.621 miles.

Knots: One knot equals 1.15 miles per hour.

Loach: The OH-6A Cayuse helicopter was a. light observation helicopter called the Loach. In 1966, the OH-6A set world records for speed, endurance, and time to climb.

Logistics Pad: Also Log Pad. The area loading supplies for delivery by helicopter, i.e., food, water, ammo.

Long and Short in Country: The day we arrived in country, i.e., 365 days, we were long in country because we had a long time to go. We counted down our tour of duty day by day. The fewer number of days left, the more experienced we were and shorter in country–closer to leaving Vietnam. One of my classmates was killed on a Friday the 13th at 1313 hours with 13 days to go.

LZ: Landing zone, the place to land a helicopter.

Mamasan: A Vietnamese woman in a position of authority. The term was corrupted to include any female worker.

Medic: Medical personnel in a combat unit or crew member on a Dustoff helicopter tasked with stabilizing wounded soldiers for transport to an evac hospital.

Mess and Mess Hall: Mess is a meal, and mess hall is a military cafeteria.

Meter: One meter equals 3 feet, 3 and 3/8 inches. One thousand meters equals one kilometer.

Montagnards: People of the Central Highlands who supported U.S. troops.

NVA: North Vietnamese Army soldiers who infiltrated into South Vietnam normally via the Ho Chi Minh Trail; industrious, deadly, persistent and capable of walking hundreds of miles for a fight.

Old Man: The commanding officer of our company; maybe 40 years old.

Papasan: A Vietnamese man in a position of authority. The term was corrupted to include any male worker.

Pay Grades (Army Ranks):
  Officers: Lieutenant through General.
  Warrant Officers: WO1 through CW4.
  Enlisted: Private through Sergeant Major.

Pedal Turn: The pilot turns the helicopter around the vertical axis with the rudder pedals at his feet.

Pierced Steel Plank: Metal planks approximately three by ten feet and pierced with holes or slits. Used to make runways and roads, and laminated with sandbags to make bunkers.

Piggyback Loads: Multiple cargo loads hung at different lengths beneath the helicopter.

Pitch: Increasing the angle of the rotor blades is "pulling pitch." It enables the helicopter to hover and fly.

Plastic Map: Maps were made of plastic to withstand wear and tear, rain and dirt.

Port Side: The left side of the aircraft.

R & R: Rest and Relaxation, our one-week holiday from the war. The farthest east we could go was Hawaii; the farthest west, Bangkok, Thailand; north, the British Colony of Hong Kong; and south, Australia.

Reserves: A military alternative to active service; held in reserve in the U.S.

Revetment: A sandbag-walled parking stall for helicopters or fixed wing aircraft.

Roll: Banking left and right; movement along the longitudinal (lengthwise) axis of the helicopter.

Satchel Charge: A demolition device made from an explosive and often covered with nails, ball bearings, or glass, and then wrapped in burlap or hidden in a satchel.

Scrip: Military personnel used paper currency; even coins were paper in Vietnam.

Short Final: Ready to land. The flight pattern consists of crosswind, downwind, base leg and final approach.

Slick: Familiar name for the UH-1 Huey as opposed to gunship for the armed version.

Sling Load: Load hung beneath the helicopter.

Sortie: A flight, a mission.

Sortie Sheet: The list of the day's missions.

South China Sea: The liquid border of Vietnam to the east.

Spooky: Air Force C-47 cargo plane converted to a gunship. The C-47 was flown in WWII, Korea, and Vietnam.

Standards Pilot: Check pilot who tested other pilots' proficiency to upgrade to aircraft commander. Also the pilot who qualified instructor pilots.

Thrust Lever: The stick mounted to the floor at the left of the pilot, called the collective stick in other helicopters

Topping Power: Power available from a turbine engine before the rotor speed begins to decrease.

Tour: Overseas assignment.

Translational Lift: Additional lift obtained from increased airspeed makes the rotor blades work more efficiently. Transition from hover to forward flight occurs at 15 to 35 knots airspeed, depending on size and weight of the helicopter.

Trip Flares: Signal flares connected to wire and set off when someone trips on the wire.

VC: Also called Viet Cong or Charlie were the local industrious, deadly, and persistent enemy.

Your Six: Covering someone's rear.

M79: A grenade launcher; the largest caliber weapon normally carried on a Chinook.

U-21: A twin engine aircraft used to transport personnel throughout Vietnam.

Authors' Bios

James V. Weatherill

Jim flew helicopters in logging operations, dam, ski lift, and power line construction as well as firefighting. He was a pilot for regional airlines and retired from a national airline as a Boeing 737 captain.

Now, he creates art from wood scraps and enjoys writing and playing his guitars. He's working on his next book, *When Paths Cross: A Novel.*

Jim is a member of the Vietnam Helicopter Pilots Assn., Vietnam Veterans of America, and Combat Helicopter Pilots Assn.

Anne Weatherill

Anne wrote for weekly and daily newspapers, and as a freelance writer published in national magazines. She also worked as a museum director and retired as a university administrative assistant. She volunteered as a Court Appointed Special Advocate and a literacy tutor.

She and Jim have two daughters and two grandsons.

Coming out 2018!!

When Paths Cross: A Novel

In summer 1973, Jayboy sat on the trunk of a wind-thrown cedar tree that sprouted when Julius Caesar was alive and died in the century Galileo was sentenced for heresies. The maelstrom that uprooted the ancient tree also sparked rebirth. The forest floor relished the space and sunlight. Eventually, seedlings took root. Now, a grove of 200-year-old youth cast spectral shadows on the ancestral corpse and the freshly dug, unmarked grave alongside.

"It was that girl and her pilot boyfriend that done it," Jayboy muttered. He ran his fingers through the tree's velvety moss shroud. Dew, trapped in the filaments, beaded on his hand. His wrist ached as he wiped his face with the cool liquid. He welcomed the pain. It reminded him of his promise. He'd find them, and he'd get them.

Paperback and e-book
Jamesweatherill.com

Made in the USA
Middletown, DE
06 August 2018